# Presidential Cookies

## The Lure and the Lore

Cookie Recipes of the Presidents of the United States

Bev Young

Edited by Ann Touryan Neumann

PRESIDENTIAL COOKIES

The Lure and the Lore

Cookie Recipes of the Presidents of the United States

by Bev Young

Published by:
Presidential Publishing
Post Office Box 221834
Sacramento, CA 95822
http:// www.presidentialcookies.com
http:// www.presidentialpublishing.com


ISBN print edition 0-9729095-3-2
First Printing 2003

Dedication: To Clint and my beloved Gato

Editor: Ann Touryan Neumann
Book Designer: Peri Poloni, Knockout Design, www.knockoutbooks.com
Cookie Photographer: Jill Withrow
Printed by: American Lithographers, Sacramento, CA

Cataloging-in-Publication Data

Young, Bev.

Presidential cookies : the lure and the lore : cookie recipes of the presidents of the United States / Bev Young ; edited by Ann Touryan Neumann.

p. cm.

Includes bibliographical references and index.

LCCN 2003102796

ISBN 0-9729095-3-2

1. Cookies--United States. 2. Presidents--United States--Biography. I. Title.

TX772.Y67 2003 641.8'654

COOKIES ON COVER: Charlottes p. 51; Double Chocolate Chip Cookies p.130; Lemon Squares p.123; Texas Governor's Mansion Cowboy Cookies p.150; Pecan Squares p.132; Sequoia Brownies p126.

PRINTED IN THE UNITED STATES OF AMERICA

# Table of Contents

# Introduction

You caught me! My hand is wrist deep in the cookie jar, so I may as well admit it: I'm addicted to cookies. Baking them as well as eating them. And certainly I am not alone. Mine is a love shared by many Americans—teething babies, Wall Street investors, too-cool teens, school teachers, real quiche-eating men, toothless seniors, a blue Sesame Street monster, football quarterbacks, Oscar winners, and even United States Presidents. Such is the lure of cookies.

I know the lure of cookies in my own house, but what was the lure of cookies in the White House? As an avid baker and muncher, I set out on a treasure hunt to find favorite cookies for each United States President. My flurry of requests to presidential libraries, museums, and historical sites brought me dozens of recipes, tips, and traditions and led to this compilation of favorite presidential cookies and presidential lore.

For over two hundred years, cookies have added sparkle and spice to White House receptions, formal dinners, and family gatherings. With each discovery of favorite presidential recipes, I uncovered curious cookie facts and stories both about the Presidents and about the role of cookies in the entertainment traditions of the First Families. The many and often little-known anecdotes about our Presidents were unexpected surprises in my cookie recipe research. These and other fun facts about our American symbols and traditions are woven throughout the cookbook, giving readers a taste of American history as well as of American cookies.

My eagerness to research these cookie recipes was surpassed only by my excitement to test bake them. Yes, I have baked *all* the recipes in *Presidential Cookies* except for a few of the early recipes, too out of date to bake. I have left those recipes in their original form. Some recipes I have fine-tuned for baking time, temperature, and ingredients, adapting them to our 21st century taste preferences. Without arm-twisting, friends and associates have been willing taste-testers, giving thumbs-up to all the presidential cookies.

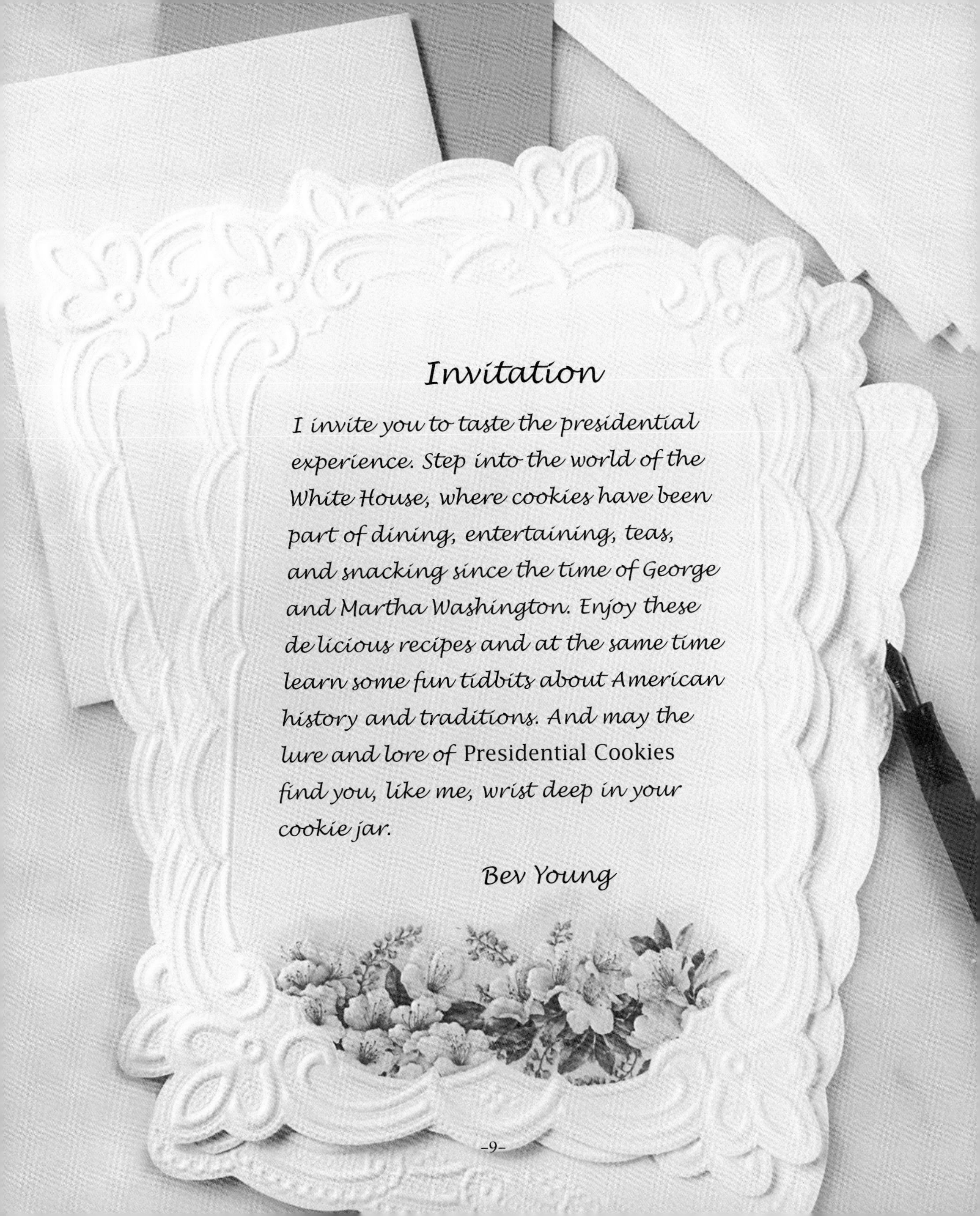

# Invitation

*I invite you to taste the presidential experience. Step into the world of the White House, where cookies have been part of dining, entertaining, teas, and snacking since the time of George and Martha Washington. Enjoy these delicious recipes and at the same time learn some fun tidbits about American history and traditions. And may the lure and lore of* Presidential Cookies *find you, like me, wrist deep in your cookie jar.*

*Bev Young*

# Cookies Then and Now

As you read *Presidential Cookies,* you will come across some original recipes taken from *The White House Cook Book* written in 1887 as well as some taken from personal presidential recipe collections and period cookbooks. While my desire was to offer original recipes of our Presidents as a reflection of history and White House tradition, recipes from our earlier Presidents often call for unusual ingredients and unusual methods of baking. Thus, I have adapted these recipes to make them easier to follow and less formidable to bake.

Ingredients, measurements, and methods for chilling dough and baking cookies have changed dramatically since the days of George Washington. Cookies in the 1700s and 1800s, called "little cakes," although simple creations, required great effort to bake. Not only were ingredients difficult to find and frequently expensive, but also preparing these basic ingredients—once obtained—required fortitude and hours of hard labor. When a recipe called for sugar, the early American baker had to knock a chunk from a fifty-five-pound sugar cone hung from the ceiling by a cord. Then he or she had to pound the chunk into granules so the sugar could be used for baking. Spices such as cinnamon sticks and nutmeg seeds required rigorous grating before the baker could add them to a recipe. With today's demands at work and at home, finding time to bake prepared cookie dough from the frozen food section of the grocery store is taxing enough.

White House cooking and baking became more convenient in the1800s when President Jefferson changed the fireplace in the White House kitchen. He had the first iron range fitted to the existing firebox. In addition, some cookie recipes from the 18th century advised the baker to be in a cool room when working with the dough since refrigerators did not exist. Eventually, perishable foods, milk, and butter were kept cold in "ice houses" with blocks of ice supplied by the "ice wagon." Then came "iceboxes," insulated boxes filled with ice that led to their name and to the popularity of Icebox Cookies. It wasn't until 1926 that the first refrigerator was installed in the White House.

Cookies grew in popularity as ingredients became available and easy to use and as refrigerators and ovens became fixtures in every American kitchen. Soon, popular ingredients such as chocolate chips and peanut butter as well as a full array of spices found their way into our cookie dough—much to our culinary delight. As you take the plunge into preparing a *Presidential Cookies* recipe, use the following cookie basic tips to help your cookies taste nothing short of presidential.

# *From the White House to Your House*

## Presidential Baking Tips

### *Getting Ready*

Read through the entire recipe first.

Preheat the oven for about fifteen minutes.

### *Gathering Ingredients*

Use only the freshest and best quality ingredients. Do not substitute ingredients.

Bring chilled ingredients, such as butter and eggs, to room temperature.

### *Gathering Equipment*

Use 9"x 13"x 1" baking pans or 8" or 9" square baking pans for bars, squares, and brownies.

Line pans with non-stick aluminum foil to prevent sticking.

Try French Silpat baking liners instead of greasing the cookie sheets.

Use parchment paper for meringues or cookies with chocolate, jam, or other ingredients that may burn.

Try using an electric mixer or food processor to chop nuts and fruit and to mix up most cookie dough instead of mixing by hand.

Use ice cream or cookie scoops for drop cookies.

Use a cookie press to make decorative shapes. Flag and star cookie cutters are great for patriotic cookies.

## *Preparing Cookie Dough*

Level flour in measuring cup with the edge of a knife.

Pack brown sugar in the measuring cup.

Spray measuring cup with a non-stick cooking spray for molasses or honey.

To beat, rapidly mix ingredients by hand or on high setting with an electric mixer.

To cream, beat butter with sugar until pale in color and smooth.

To blend, mix ingredients by hand or on the lowest setting of an electric mixer.

Beat egg whites with an electric mixer set on high. Gently fold ingredients into beaten egg whites so whites stay airy with stiff peaks.

Add oats, nuts, coconut, chocolate chips, and chopped fruits by hand after the cookie dough has been mixed.

Lightly flour the rolling pin as well as the cookie cutters when rolling out dough and cutting out shapes.

When specified, chill cookie dough well before slicing or cutting into shapes.

Do not over-mix cookie dough or cookies will be tough.

## *Baking Cookies*

Place rolled cookies about 1 inch apart on the cookie sheet. Place dropped cookies about 2 inches apart.

Bake several test cookies to determine the correct oven temperature, baking time, and space needed between cookies on the cookie sheet.

Place cookies on a cookie sheet that is room temperature. Do not place them on a hot sheet just out of the oven.

Bake cookies one sheet at a time in the middle of the oven for evenly baked cookies.

Bake bars, squares, and brownies in the specified pan size. Otherwise, they will be under- or over-baked.

Cool cookies briefly on the cookie sheet to allow them to firm up a little. Then remove them to a wire rack to cool completely.

Slice shortbread while it is still slightly warm.

## *Decorating Cookies*

Decorate cut-out or press cookies.

Use colored sugars, a cinnamon-sugar mixture, or rainbow sprinkles on cookies before or after baking.

Lightly paint cookies with corn syrup after cooling baked cookies and then dip in colored sugar.

Pipe icing on cookies from a pastry bag or tubes purchased at the grocery store.

Add nuts or chopped fruit.

Drizzle white or dark melted chocolate on top of baked cookies.

## *Freezing and Storing Cookies*

Freeze most cookie dough, except meringues, ladyfingers, and macaroons, several weeks before baking if desired. Tightly seal the dough in batch amounts and freeze.

Defrost a batch in the refrigerator before baking.

Store baked soft cookies in an airtight container or sealed plastic bag.

Keep baked crisp cookies in a loosely covered container where air can circulate.

Store varieties of baked cookies separately so that the flavors do not mix.

Freeze baked cookies for several weeks. Freeze them individually on a cookie sheet. Then put them in a sealed plastic bag or cover them well with plastic wrap and foil. Defrost at room temperature. Then microwave them for a few seconds to restore the almost out-of-the-oven taste and aroma.

## *Gift Giving and Mailing Ideas*

Consider mailing only sturdy cookies, such as bar cookies, brownies (without icing), and dropped or pressed cookies. Wrap cookies for freshness.

Make a nostalgic *Presidential Cookies* sampler for tastes of a by-gone era.

Create fancy festive cutouts for parties, gifts, and holidays.

Serve cookies on a plate decorated with a red, white, and blue color theme and flags.

# George Washington (1732-1799)

## 1st President of the United States

(1789-1797)

GEORGE WASHINGTON

MARTHA WASHINGTON

George Washington and his wife, Martha, affectionately called Lady Washington, established the first presidential entertainment traditions with their teas, receptions, and banquets. Born and raised on American soil but still steeped in British tradition, President Washington held formal receptions in the President's House in New York and Philadelphia. The White House in Washington, D.C., had not yet been built.

The President's receptions, called levees, were an old English court custom. Their formality emphasized the new republic's parity with European governments and the authority of the presidency. Invited dignitaries, dressed in tailcoats, ruffled collars, silver buckles, and powdered hair, arrived at the levees. They bowed one by one before President Washington as they took their places in seats assembled in a circle. The President then walked around the circle, speaking briefly to each guest. He also bowed but never shook hands.

Despite the formality of the levees, President and Mrs. Washington welcomed their visitors with warm hospitality and served them simple food. Guests could help themselves to cookies, candies, tea, cake, coffee, and lemonade.

While the President held his reception for gentlemen every Tuesday from three to four o'clock in the afternoon, Lady Washington invited both men and women guests on Friday evenings at seven o'clock. In 1790, New Year's Day fell on Friday, the day of Lady Washington's weekly gathering. To celebrate the holiday, the Washingtons combined their two receptions that week, holding them both on New Year's Day, from twelve o'clock to three in the afternoon.

At this first New Year's Day celebration, the Washingtons served cookies and cakes along with Cherry Bounce, a drink made from spirits and sour cherries. So began the presidential tradition to hold a reception every New Year's Day. Favorite cookies of President and Lady Washington, such as Shrewsbury Cakes and Jumbals, may have been served at the New Year's Day receptions and at the Washingtons' presidential receptions.

The Christmas season had special meaning for the President and Lady Washington, who had married during the winter holiday. Whenever possible, they tried to spend the holiday together. Lady Washington traveled in bitter weather during the Revolutionary War to be with her husband each winter. After retiring from their presidential duties, the Washingtons returned to their home, Mount Vernon. They continued to entertain frequently, especially during the Christmas holiday.

One possible specialty at Mount Vernon was Shrewsbury Cakes (spelled Shrowsbury in early American English). The origins of Shrewsbury Cakes date back to English recipes more than four hundred years old. The following is a modern version of Martha Washington's "receipt," the word for recipe during her days.

## PRESIDENTIAL SEAL

**The official seal of the President of the United States displays the American eagle. It carries in its beak a scroll with the Latin words, *E Pluribus Unum* (Out of Many, One). This phrase represents the idea that from many states comes one nation. The original seal had thirteen stars for the thirteen colonies, and the eagle faced the thirteen arrows of war. In 1945, President Truman had the Presidential Seal and Flag redesigned. He had the eagle's head turned toward the olive branch of peace and added 48 stars to stand for each state in the Union at that time.**

# Shrewsbury Cakes

*The dried cherries, apricots, or currants give these tender round cakes a sweet fruit flavor.*

1/2 CUP SOFT BUTTER (1 STICK)
1/2 CUP SUGAR
1/2 TSP. VANILLA
1/4 TSP. SALT
1 EGG, BEATEN
2 1/2 CUPS SIFTED CAKE FLOUR
ABOUT 1 CUP DRIED FRUIT (TART DRIED CHERRIES, APRICOTS, OR CURRANTS), CHOPPED

1. Preheat oven to 350°.
2. Cream butter with sugar.
3. Add vanilla, salt, and egg and blend.
4. Add flour.
5. Mix in dried fruit.
6. Chill dough for about one hour.
7. Use a small cookie scoop to form small rounds.
8. Place rounds on a greased cookie sheet.
9. Bake for about 12 minutes.
10. Cool on a rack.

YIELD: 3 DOZEN CAKES.

*On March 4, 1793 at his second inauguration, George Washington delivered the shortest inaugural speech, containing only 135 words.*

# Jumbals

*In early American baking, various cookies were called Jumbals, sometimes spelled Jumballs or Jumbles. They were another favorite cookie of President and Lady Washington during the Christmas season. The following is an adaptation of 18th century Jumbals.*

1 CUP BUTTER (2 STICKS)
1 CUP SUGAR
1/4 TSP. SALT
GRATED RIND OF 1 ORANGE
1 EGG, WELL-BEATEN
3 CUPS SIFTED FLOUR

1. Preheat oven to 350°.
2. In a large bowl, cream butter, sugar, salt, and rind until light and fluffy.
3. Beat in egg.
4. Add flour, working it thoroughly into dough.
5. Sprinkle sugar on a surface and shape small pieces of the dough into little rolls.
6. Join ends to make rings 1 1/2 inches across.
7. Bake on greased cookie sheet until brown about 10 to 15 minutes.
8. Cool on a rack.

YIELD: 5 DOZEN JUMBALS.

**MOUNT VERNON**
*West View*
*Painting attributed to Edward Savage, c. 1792*

**The Mount Vernon Ladies' Association (MVLA) has maintained Mount Vernon without government funding since just before the Civil War, relying instead solely on private donations. The MVLA is the first national preservation organization in the United States.**

*Mount Vernon kitchen*

# John Adams (1735-1826)

## 2nd President of the United States

(1797-1801)

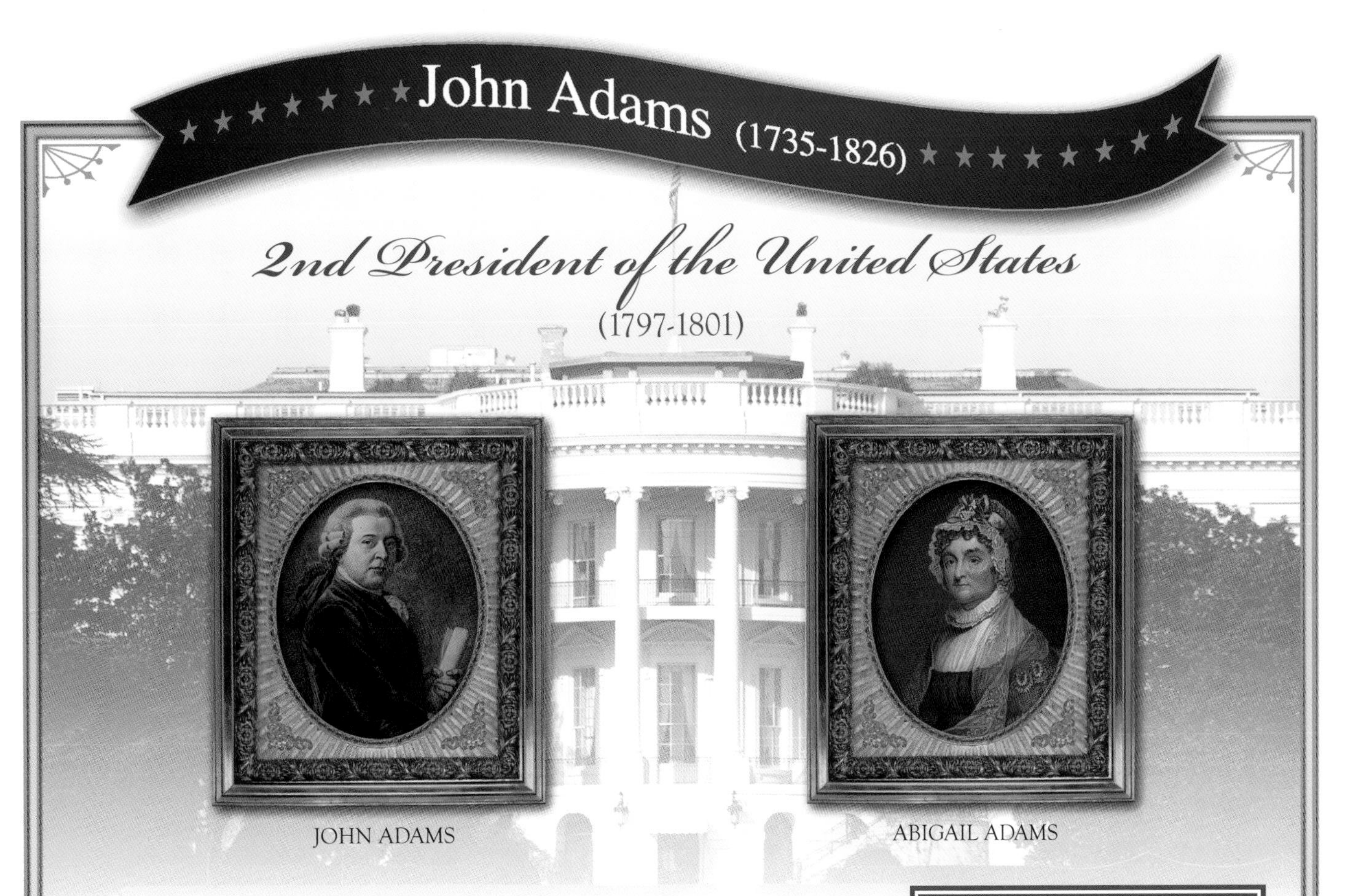

JOHN ADAMS

ABIGAIL ADAMS

President John and First Lady Abigail Adams were the first residents of the newly built White House, known initially as the "President's Palace." Although construction of the White House was far from complete, the President and First Lady offered the most ceremonious hospitality possible under the circumstances.

On New Year's Day, 1801, they formally opened the mansion's massive doors with a grand reception. White House staff mixed batters for dozens of rich cakes, regional cookies, and dainty tarts and baked them in the new ovens of the massive kitchen fireplace. Were you one of the honored guests, you might be sipping a frothy syllabub and sampling custard topped with meringue, known as floating island. Your china plate would be piled with fancy curds, creams, trifles, jellies, fruits, and sweetmeats so popular in the Adamses' days. The United States Marine Band would be playing patriotic tunes.

### WHITE HOUSE

The White House has been called the President's Palace, President's House, People's House, and the Executive Mansion. As early as 1812, it was given the nickname "The White House," probably because of its protective whitewash. In 1901, President Teddy Roosevelt made the name official. The White House is now the oldest official residence of a head of state anywhere in the world.

An essential ingredient in early American cooking and White House cuisine was molasses. Stout, dark molasses was used to sweeten such desserts as rich ginger cookies and gingerbread because sugar was very expensive. John Adams considered molasses an essential ingredient in American independence, a reference to the Molasses Act of 1733. The British Parliament had passed the Act to tax sugar and molasses imported into the colonies from the West Indies and to impose shipment restrictions. The tax levied by this act is considered one of the indirect economic reasons for the American Revolution. True to President Adams's reference to molasses as an "essential ingredient," the following recipe for Brandy Snaps is rich with the thick syrup.

**John Adams wrote about Independence Day:**

***"It ought to be solemnized with pomp and parade, with shows, games, sports, guns, bells, bonfires, and illuminations, from one end of this continent to the other, from this time forward for evermore."***

# Brandy Snaps

1 cup butter (2 sticks)
1 cup sugar
1 cup light molasses
1 Tbsp. brandy
1 tsp. ginger
1 3/4 cups sifted flour
Powdered sugar for dusting

1. Preheat oven to 325°.
2. In a medium saucepan, heat butter, sugar, molasses, and brandy until well blended.
3. Add ginger.
4. Remove mixture from heat and add the flour a little at a time, beating after each addition.
5. Drop teaspoons of the mixture onto a greased cookie sheet, allowing 3 inches between the snaps for spreading.
6. Bake 8 to 12 minutes.
7. Cool snaps on a rack.
8. Dust lightly with powdered sugar.

Yield: 4 dozen snaps.

*Until the last decade, Adams was noted for living longer than any other President. He lived to be 90 years, 247 days old. This distinction is now granted to former President Ronald Reagan.*

# Thomas Jefferson (1743-1826)

## 3rd President of the United States

(1801-1809)

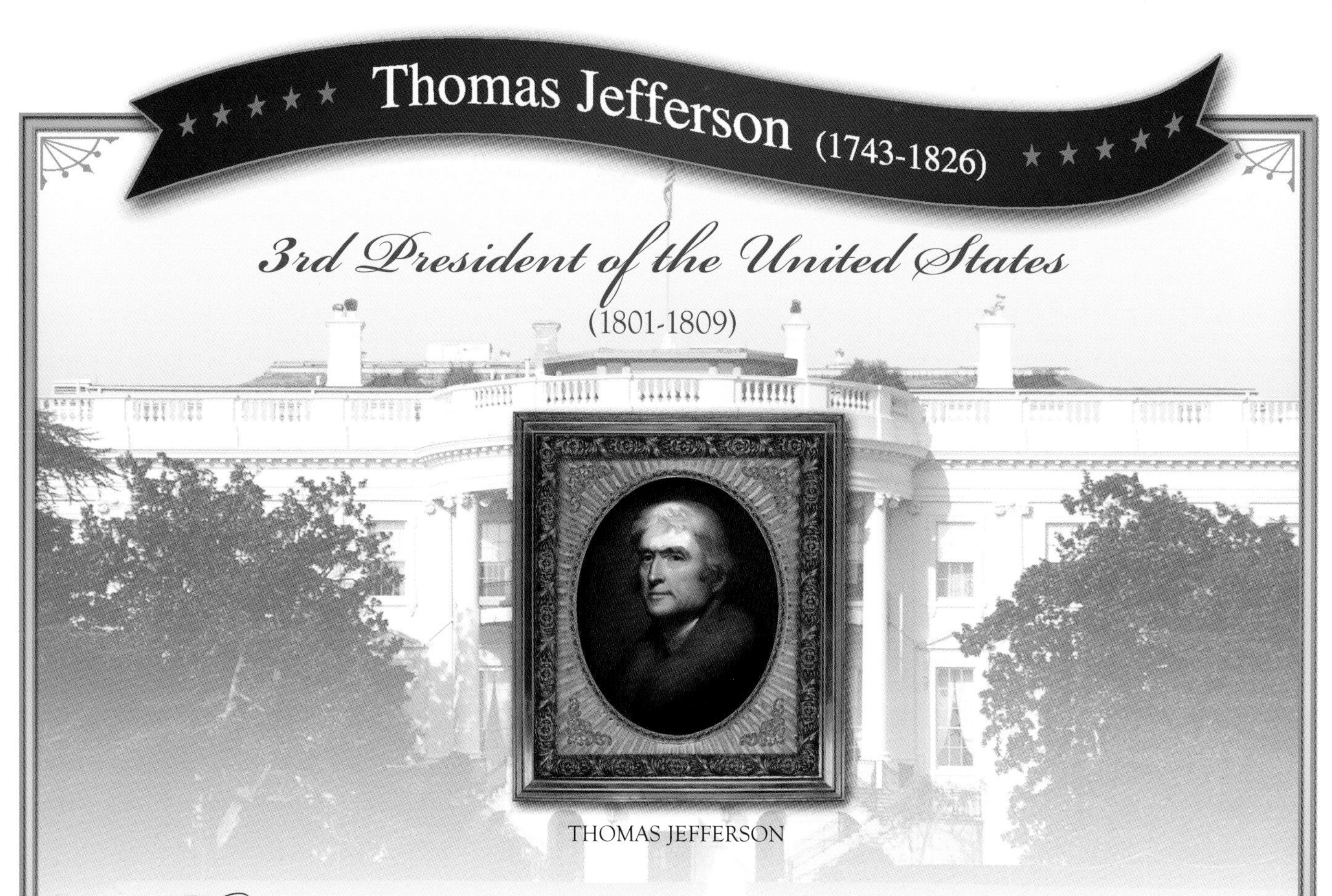

THOMAS JEFFERSON

President Thomas Jefferson was renowned for lavish entertaining both at the White House and at his home, Monticello. He held the first inaugural open house in 1805. Many people who had attended the swearing-in ceremony at the United States Capitol followed him to the White House, where he entertained them in the Blue Room. As it had done at Jefferson's first inauguration, the United States Marine Band performed its versatile repertoire of bright marches and patriotic music. Jefferson designated the band "The President's Own." It has played regularly at the presidential inaugurations and exclusively for White House events ever since.

A widower, Jefferson hosted executive galas with help from his daughters, Martha and Mary. On some occasions, he also called on Dolley Madison to step in as White House hostess.

In a democratic spirit, Jefferson welcomed the public to annual receptions on New Year's Day and on the Fourth of July. He also opened the "People's House," as he called the White House, for public tours, replacing the formal presidential bow with a simple handshake when greeting visitors.

Jefferson's presidential dinners gained notoriety for their opulence and abundance. These sumptuous meals were often capped off by many desserts. Jefferson served meringues, macaroons, quaking jellies, and flummery, a popular custard of his era. He also introduced his guests to tantalizing desserts he had sampled in Europe, such as blanc-mange and crème brulee.

# Coconut Macaroons

*Jefferson apparently enjoyed macaroons. This recipe is an updated recipe for macaroons using sweet coconut.*

1/4 TSP. SALT
1 EGG WHITE
1 CUP SUGAR
1 CUP ROLLED OATS
1/4 CUP GRATED SWEETENED COCONUT
1/2 TSP. VANILLA

1. Preheat oven to 350°.
2. Add salt to egg white and beat until stiff, adding sugar gradually and beating constantly.
3. Fold in rolled oats, coconut, and vanilla, mixing well.
4. Drop from a teaspoon onto a greased cookie sheet.
5. Bake for 12 minutes.

YIELD: 2 DOZEN MACAROONS.

*Jefferson was the first President to be inaugurated in Washington, D.C.*

*Jefferson sold about 6,000 books from his private library to help start the Library of Congress.*

*At the age of thirty-three, Jefferson drafted the Declaration of Independence.*

# James Madison (1751-1836)

## *4th President of the United States*

(1809-1817)

JAMES MADISON

DOLLEY MADISON

With his dignified charm and her sparkling wit, President James and First Lady Dolley Madison captured the hearts of Washington's socially elite, both during and after their time in the White House. Dolley Madison's vivaciousness and social flair earned her the title "Lady Presidentess." She would turn even the most routine event into a festive occasion.

The Madisons' zest for entertaining had delighted guests even before they took up residence in the White House. Dolley Madison had often served as hostess for Thomas Jefferson during his term as President, bestowing her engaging hospitality on Washington society well before her husband was elected in 1809.

Once in the White House, First Lady Dolley established weekly festive receptions called "drawing

### JAMES MADISON

– was the first President to wear trousers rather than knee breeches.

– was also the shortest President at 5 feet, 4 inches.

During Madison's administration,

– Social dancing was introduced at the White House. Critics at the time called it "the hugging process set to music."

– In 1814, Francis Scott Key wrote "The Star-Spangled Banner."

### DOLLEY MADISON

– sent the first personal message using the Morse telegraph in 1844.

– was granted the highest honor ever given a President's widow when she was voted a lifetime seat on the floor of the House of Representatives.

During the war with the British, Dolley Madison turned her spyglass in every direction from the roof of the White House, watching the invading British troops. When within the sound of cannons, Mrs. Madison gathered as many government papers as she could and fled for safety. At the last moment, she told her staff to retrieve the portrait of George Washington. With no time left, they broke the frame, grabbed the portrait to save it from destruction, and escaped. When the British entered the White House, they sat down and ate the dinner that the First Lady had prepared and then set the mansion ablaze.

rooms." She also gave "dove parties" for the Cabinet wives to ensure that while their husbands consulted with the President, they were having fun. To make all the guests visiting the President feel welcome, the First Lady personally offered refreshments to each, turning their business appointments with her husband into memorable and delectable occasions.

In 1814, British troops marched on Washington and set fire to the White House, forcing the President and First Lady to move into temporary living quarters. Despite smaller quarters, the Madisons' parties continued. These parties were so popular, with guests crowding into the rooms until almost unable to move, that they were called "Mrs. Madison's squeezes."

No cookbooks for the Madisons have been preserved. However, the following recipe for Apple Date Nut Brownies is taken from *Montpelier Hospitality*, a cookbook filled with the history and traditions of the Madisons' home, Montpelier, and with recipes compiled by the volunteers at Montpelier and The Montpelier Foundation. These brownies—made with apples, dates, and a simmered buttery-brown sugar mixture—would have been worthy of a nod of approval from Dolley Madison herself had she nibbled one.

*View from the northeast of the fire-damaged White House, called at the time the President's Palace.*

# Apple Date Nut Brownies

1-POUND BOX DARK BROWN SUGAR
3/4 CUP BUTTER (1 1/2 STICKS)
2 EGGS
2 TBSP. VANILLA
2 MEDIUM COOKING APPLES, PEELED, CORED, AND CHOPPED
2 1/2 CUPS ALL-PURPOSE FLOUR
2 TSP. BAKING POWDER
1/2 TSP. SALT
1/2 CUP CHOPPED PECANS
1/2 CUP CHOPPED DATES

1. Preheat oven to 350°.
2. Combine sugar and butter in a large saucepan.
3. Cook over low heat, stirring constantly until sugar dissolves.
4. Remove saucepan from heat and cool to room temperature.
5. Beat in eggs and add vanilla.
6. In a small bowl, toss apples with 1/4 cup of the flour and set aside.
7. Add remaining 2 1/4 cups flour, baking powder, and salt to sugar mixture and mix well.
8. Fold in apples, pecans, and dates.
9. Pour into a greased 15 x 10 x 1-inch jelly-roll pan.
10. Bake for 35 minutes or until a toothpick stuck in the center comes out clean.
11. Cool completely before cutting into squares.

YIELD: 2 TO 3 DOZEN BROWNIES.

*A serving suggestion*

For a grand finale dessert, place a scoop of vanilla or butter pecan ice cream on each brownie. Then drizzle warm caramel ice cream sauce over the top.

# James Monroe (1758-1831)

## 5th President of the United States

(1817-1825)

JAMES MONROE

ELIZABETH MONROE

While in the White House, President James and First Lady Elizabeth Monroe polished social and political occasions with a fine dusting of French style. They were accustomed to the formality and elegance of French society, for they had lived in Paris while James Monroe served as the United States Minister to France. Their desire to imitate the entertainment style of European courts was reflected in their receptions. Servants offered dainty sweets and tiny cakes along with slender glasses of wine on silver trays to guests as they warmed themselves by the giant White House fireplaces.

***During the Monroe administration, Congress set the number of stripes on the United States flag at 13 to honor the original colonies.***

***Monroe was the first President to ride on a steamboat.***

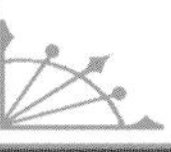

# Waverly Jumbles

*The Monroes often served Waverly Jumbles. This 1800's recipe from the* Monroe Family Recipes *cookbook is unusually simple and short.*

### HISTORIC RECIPE

One pound of flour; one-half pound of butter; three-fourths pound of brown sugar; two eggs; one-half teaspoon of nutmeg; two tablespoons of rose water. Roll out long and cut into strips; join into rings and bake.

*A modern adaptation of Waverly Jumbles follows. Bakers enjoyed the floral flavoring of rosewater in their baking until the 19th century when vanilla flavoring became popular. However, rosewater can still be purchased in many grocery and specialty food stores.*

1 CUP BUTTER (2 STICKS)
2 CUPS LIGHT BROWN SUGAR, PACKED
2 EGGS
2 TBSP. ROSEWATER OR 2 TSP. VANILLA
4 CUPS FLOUR
1/2 TSP. NUTMEG

1. Preheat oven to 350°.
2. In a large bowl, cream the butter and sugar together completely.
3. Beat in eggs and flavoring.
4. Stir in flour.
5. Chill the dough for one hour or longer.
6. Pinch off a piece of dough and roll it into a 2-inch rope.
7. Join the ends to form a ring.
8. Bake the rings for 10 to 12 minutes.
9. Cool on a rack.

YIELD: 5 DOZEN JUMBLES.

# Cry Babies

*The Monroes were from Virginia where Cry Babies originated. The cookies' curious name comes from a typical African tradition on plantations–to give vivid, unusual names to dishes and desserts. Perhaps to quell the sobs of tired youngsters on the plantations, parents treated their children to Cry Babies. These cookies, which may have been baked for the Monroes, combine the richness of molasses with ingredients from an old English recipe.*

1/2 CUP SUGAR
1/2 CUP MOLASSES, LIGHT OR DARK
1/2 CUP BUTTER (1 STICK)
1 EGG, SLIGHTLY BEATEN
1 1/2 TSP. GINGER
1/4 TSP. SALT
3/8 CUP BOILING WATER
1 1/2 TSP. BAKING SODA
ABOUT 2 CUPS FLOUR

1. Preheat oven to 375°.
2. In a large bowl, mix together sugar, molasses, and butter.
3. Add slightly beaten egg, ginger, salt, boiling water, and baking soda.
4. Mix together thoroughly.
5. Stir in flour, just enough to make a somewhat stiff batter.
6. Drop by teaspoon onto a greased cookie sheet at least 2 inches apart, allowing room for the "babies" to spread.
7. Bake about 10 minutes, or until the touch of your finger leaves no mark.
8. Cool on a rack.

YIELD: 3 DOZEN CRY BABIES.

# John Quincy Adams (1767-1848)

## 6th President of the United States

(1825-1829)

JOHN QUINCY ADAMS

LOUISA ADAMS

*It is believed that "Yankee Doodle," the song that rallied American revolutionaries, has as many as 190 verses.*

President John Quincy and First Lady Louisa Adams continued the formal entertaining style of the Monroes. However, they chose to greet their guests in a personal fashion, moving from group to group to briefly chat. Their receptions, called "drawing rooms," included roasted coffees, East Indian tea, imported liquors, and a variety of cakes, jellies, ice cream, and fruit from the West Indies. They served cookies, often called "little cakes," with punch or wine at both drawing rooms and official receptions. Ginger and molasses, chief ingredients of most desserts of the era, give these Soft Molasses Cakes their spiciness and soft texture.

# Soft Molasses Cakes

*This adapted early American recipe was popular during Adams's presidency.*

1 cup soft butter (2 sticks)
1 1/2 cups molasses, light or dark
1/4 cup sugar
4 cups flour
1 1/2 tsp. salt
2 tsp. baking soda
2 tsp. cinnamon
1 1/2 tsp. ground ginger
1/2 tsp. cloves
1 egg

1. Preheat oven to 350°.
2. In a large bowl, sift together flour, salt, baking soda, cinnamon, ground ginger, and cloves. Set aside.
3. In a large saucepan melt butter. Stir in sugar and molasses and cool.
4. Mix a small amount of flour mixture into the melted butter mixture.
5. Beat in egg.
6. Add remaining flour and blend until smooth.
7. Chill dough for about 2 hours.
8. Shape into small balls and place on a cookie sheet about 2 inches apart.
9. Bake for about 15 minutes.
10. Remove to a rack to cool.

Yield: 6 dozen cakes.

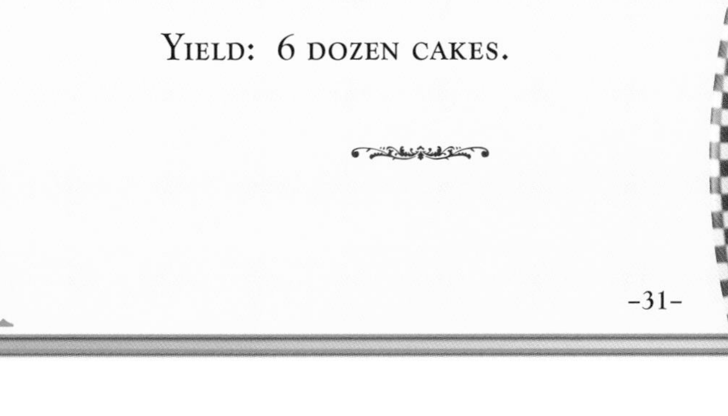

# Andrew Jackson (1767-1845)

## 7th President of the United States

(1829-1837)

ANDREW JACKSON

> A widower when he assumed office, Jackson was the only President who served in both the Revolutionary War and the War of 1812.
>
> Jackson was the first President
>
> – to be born in a log cabin.
>
> – to ride on a railroad train.

Nicknamed "Old Hickory" by his troops for being "tough as hickory" in the War of 1812, President Andrew Jackson was known as the first frontier President. Elected by popular vote, Jackson wanted the public to see his election as a victory for the people. His presidency began and ended with raucous receptions. After his swearing-in ceremony, he planned a private celebration indoors as well as an inaugural reception outdoors on the White House lawn. However, a throng of more than twenty thousand people followed the President back to the White House. They poured inside for the refreshments, ice cream, punch, cakes, and ices. Unfortunately, the excited, shoving crowd behaved badly, gobbling up everything in sight. In the frenzy, they broke china and glasses. They even stood on the elegant furniture just to get at the food and beverages. In desperation, staff carried tubs of punch and ice cream outside to lure the eager spectators out of the White House.

*This drawing, titled President's Levee or All Creation Going to the White House, depicts the crowd in front of the White House during Andrew Jackson's first inaugural reception in 1829.*

President Jackson's administration ended with a comparable fiasco. Presented with a 1400-pound cheese—four feet in diameter and three feet thick—President Jackson decided to hold a final reception, called a levee, to share the cheese with the public. He announced that all were welcome to attend and enjoy "the cheese." The result was bedlam. Crowds swarmed the White House to get a sample. The huge cheese was devoured in several hours, but aromatic reminders of it were left for months.

Children, cookies, and frivolity were also part of Jackson's entertainment style. During one Christmas holiday, President Jackson sent notes to about one hundred children of Washington, D.C., which read: "The children of President Jackson's family request you to join them on Christmas Day, at four o'clock p.m., in a frolic in the East Room." Once the children arrived, White House staff served the young guests a holiday feast, including lots of desserts. The dining table's centerpiece, a pyramid of starched cotton snowballs, added to the children's Christmas frolic. After supper, President Jackson gave the snowballs to the children, who were then allowed to have a snowball toss in the East Room.

In keeping with holiday traditions of previous Presidents, Jackson opened the White House on New Year's Day for all who wanted to come and greet him. As in earlier administrations, wine and "little cakes" tantalized guests. The following recipes are some cookies popular during Jackson's time that may have been among his favorites.

# Benne Cakes

*Jackson may have offered his guests delicacies such as these "cakes" made from benne (sesame) seeds.*

*The Africans who brought benne seeds to this country considered them good luck. While African Americans used them as we now use chocolate chips, munched in handfuls or mixed into desserts, other Americans slowly began to enjoy their distinctive flavor, using them in candies, pies, and cookies.*

3/4 cup butter (1 1/2 sticks)
1/2 cup sugar
Grated rind of 1 orange
1 egg
1/2 cup milk
3 cups flour
2 tsp. baking powder
1/2 tsp. salt
1/2 tsp. nutmeg

1. Preheat oven to 350°.
2. In a large bowl, cream butter with sugar until light and fluffy.
3. Stir in the grated orange rind.
4. In a small bowl, beat egg slightly with milk. Set aside.
5. In a third bowl, sift flour with baking powder, salt, and nutmeg.
6. Alternately add the flour mixture and the egg-milk mixture to the sugar and butter.
7. Put a little flour on your hands, pinch off pieces of the dough, and roll them into little balls about the size of a walnut.
8. Bake on an ungreased cookie sheet for about 10 minutes or until delicately browned.
9. Cool on a rack.

Glaze
3/4 cup honey
2 Tbsp. butter
3 Tbsp. benne (sesame) seeds

To Glaze:

1. Cook honey, butter, and 3 tablespoons benne seeds in a pan until a few test drops separate into hard threads in cold water (about 200° on a candy thermometer).
2. Cool until the foam settles.
3. Dip the top of each cookie in the glaze.
4. Work quickly because the glaze hardens fast. If the glaze becomes unworkable, reheat the glaze over hot water.
5. Stir to keep the seeds from rising to the top.

Yield: 5 dozen cakes.

*The Great Cheese Levee*
*Citizens help devour an enormous cheese*
Perley's Reminiscences

**During Jackson's presidency,**

**– The estate of James Smithson funded the Smithsonian Institution for "the increase and diffusion of knowledge." The Smithsonian is one of the world's largest research organizations. Over 140 million items can be found in the Institution's museums.**

**– Samuel F. Smith wrote "My Country Tis of Thee."**

**– Running water was piped into the White House.**

# Beaten Sweet Cakes

2 cups butter (4 sticks)
2 cups sugar
2 eggs, slightly beaten
4 cups sifted flour
1 cup chopped nuts, any variety

1. Preheat oven to 350°.
2. Cream butter with sugar.
3. Add 2 slightly beaten eggs and beat vigorously.
4. Add sifted flour. Mix well.
5. Put the dough on a floured surface and knead thoroughly.
6. Work in nuts.
7. Roll out the dough and cut into shapes.
8. Place cookies on a greased cookie sheet and bake 12 to15 minutes.
9. Cool on a rack.

Yield: 5 dozen Sweet Cakes.

# Martin Van Buren (1782-1862)

## *8th President of the United States*

(1837-1841)

MARTIN VAN BUREN

> Van Buren was the first President born a citizen of the United States. All previous Presidents were born in the colonies before 1776, the year the nation officially became the United States of America.
>
> Van Buren painted the White House oval salon a rich blue. The room became known as the "blue room."

As soon as President Martin Van Buren took office in 1837, he began to refurbish the White House, which had become tattered from public use during Jackson's term. A thorough scrub of the White House, stylish re-upholstery on the furniture, and purchases of new rugs, china, and glassware renewed the elegance of the White House and brightened the social affairs of the presidency. President Martin Van Buren preferred small dinner parties for a select group of friends to large formal receptions. A widower, he enlisted his daughter-in-law, Angelica, to serve as hostess at his social events.

Although from New York, President Van Buren was of Dutch heritage and quite possibly served Dutch "koekjes" or cookies at White House teas. Dutch settlers had brought koekjes to the colonies. The settlers baked them in molds with imprints, such as an eagle or the name of a famous person. They ate these tasty molded cookies with their wine or tea. The Dutch also had a unique way of drinking their tea. They placed a lump of sugar between their teeth as they sipped the hot tea, the sugar melting gradually in their mouths. President Van Buren may have enjoyed his koekjes while sipping his tea in this fashion.

# Dutch Koekjes

*These cookies must be prepared the day before baking.*

2 CUPS BUTTER (4 STICKS)
2 CUPS SUGAR
4 CUPS SIFTED FLOUR
4 TSP. CINNAMON
1/2 TSP. NUTMEG
1/2 TSP. CLOVES
1/2 TSP. BAKING SODA
1/4 TSP. SALT
1/2 CUP SOUR CREAM
1/2 CUP CHOPPED NUTS, ANY VARIETY

*The term "O.K." originated with Van Buren. He was from Kinderhook, New York, which was often referred to as Old Kinderhook. Groups called O.K. Clubs supported Van Buren's campaign. "O.K." later came to mean "all right."*

1. Preheat oven to 400°.
2. In a large bowl, cream butter with sugar.
3. In another bowl, sift flour with spices, salt, and soda.
4. Add sifted flour alternately with sour cream to creamed mixture.
5. Add nuts.
6. Knead together well.
7. Shape into a roll about 2 inches in diameter, wrap in plastic wrap, and chill in the refrigerator overnight.
8. Slice, place rounds on an ungreased cookie sheet, and bake until browned, about 10 to 12 minutes.

YIELD: 6 DOZEN KOEKJES.

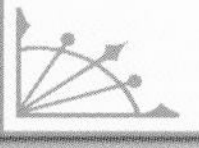

# William Henry Harrison (1773-1841)

## 9th President of the United States

(1841)

WILLIAM HENRY HARRISON

ANNA HARRISON

Harrison's father was one of the signers of the Declaration of Independence.

Harrison was a clerk of Hamilton County Court, Ohio, immediately before becoming President.

Anna Harrison was the only First Lady to become the grandmother of a President: Benjamin Harrison.

The administration of President William Henry Harrison lasted just one month. Although he delivered the longest inaugural address of 8,445 words on March 4, 1841, he served the shortest term of any United States President. Popular cookies during his era were these lemony Hospitality Thins.

# Hospitality Thins

*The original recipe directed the baker to flatten these cookies with a cookie stamp to create thins. The following adaptation results in more flavorful, soft, lemony mounds. Lightly dust them with powdered sugar.*

2/3 cup soft butter (1 stick + 5 1/3 Tbsp.)
1 cup sugar
2 tsp. grated lemon rind
2 tsp. ginger
1/2 tsp. baking soda
1/2 tsp. salt
1 tsp. vanilla
1 egg
2 Tbsp. lemon juice
2 cups sifted flour
Powdered sugar to dust cookies

1. Preheat oven to 400°.
2. In a large bowl, cream butter and sugar together.
3. Add lemon rind, ginger, baking soda, salt, and vanilla.
4. Beat in egg and lemon juice.
5. Stir in flour and mix well.
6. Refrigerate dough for 2 hours or more.
7. Shape into 3/4-inch balls.
8. Place 1 1/2 inches apart on ungreased cookie sheets.
9. Bake 6 to 8 minutes until set but not hard.
10. Let cookies cool for about 30 seconds.
11. Cool completely on a rack.
12. Dust with powdered sugar.

Yield: 6 dozen thins.

# John Tyler (1790-1862)

## *10th President of the United States*

(1841-1845)

LETITIA TYLER JOHN TYLER JULIA TYLER

> ***Within one year, 1841, Martin Van Buren, William Henry Harrison, and John Tyler served as President.***

President John Tyler became the first President to marry while in office. After the death of First Lady Letitia, he met and married Julia Gardiner, a beautiful woman thirty years younger than the President. The new First Lady brought regal splendor to White House entertaining during the last months of President Tyler's administration. At formal receptions, First Lady Julia welcomed guests atop a large armchair placed on a platform. Elegantly dressed with plumes in her hair, she then strolled about the banquet rooms, attended by maids of honor dressed in white.

Gaiety flourished at White House events, the Tylers introducing the polka to Washington society. First Lady Julia requested that the United States Marine Band play "Hail to the Chief" whenever her husband entered the room for official functions. This musical tradition continues to this day when a President appears at a state function. At the Tylers' last dinner party, given for the President-elect and Mrs. Polk, First Lady Julia wore around her neck a golden pen. It was the pen that her husband had used to sign the treaty that made Texas part of the Union.

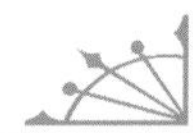

# Geneva Wafers

*Appearing in* The White House Cook Book, *1887 Edition, this recipe is described as creating "a very pretty and ornamental dish for the supper table, and is very nice, and very easily made." A popular recipe of the era, these whipped-cream-filled wafers might have added a bit of elegance to the Tylers' receptions.*

## HISTORIC RECIPE

Two eggs, three ounces of butter, three ounces of flour, three ounces of pounded sugar. Well whisk the eggs, put them a basin, and stir into them the butter, which should be beaten to a cream; add the flour and sifted sugar gradually, and then mix all well together. Butter a baking sheet, and drop on it a teaspoonful of the mixture at a time, leaving a space between each. Bake in a cool oven; watch the pieces of paste, and when half done, roll them up like wafers, and put in a small wedge of bread or piece of wood to keep them in shape. Return them to the oven until crisp. Before serving, remove the bread, put a spoonful of preserves in the widest end, and fill up with whipped cream.

*The historic recipe for Geneva Wafers is quite possibly the forerunner of Cream Cones that also uses preserves and whipped cream.*

# Cream Cones

1/3 cup butter or margarine (5 1/2 Tbsp.)
1/3 cup sugar
1/2 cup sifted all-purpose flour
4 egg whites
Preserves
1/2 cup heavy cream (canned whipped cream may be substituted for the cream and sugar)
3 Tbsp. sugar

1. Preheat oven to 400°.
2. Melt butter.
3. Stir in sugar and flour, blending until smooth.
4. Beat the egg whites until they are stiff.
5. Fold egg whites into the butter and flour mixture.
6. Drop batter from a tablespoon onto a hot, well-greased baking sheet, spacing well apart.
7. Bake only 2 or 3 cones at a time.
8. Spread each mound into a paper-thin oblong about 4 or 5 inches long.
9. Bake about 5 minutes or until deep golden brown.
10. Quickly remove and roll into cones while hot.
11. Continue until batter is used.
12. Whip heavy cream with sugar.
13. Fill bottom of cooled cones with the preserves.
14. Fill the large ends of the cones with the whipped cream piped through a pastry tube.
15. Refrigerate cones if they are not eaten immediately.

Yield: 10 Cream Cones.

# James Polk (1795-1849)

JAMES POLK

SARAH POLK

When entertaining, President James and First Lady Sarah Polk were less extravagant than their predecessors. They did not always offer food and drink at official receptions. When the Polks did offer refreshments to guests, they often served grape pyramids, ice cream, and ladyfingers. Meals were kept simple, reflecting the tastes of the First Family and their desire to live within their budget. The Polks are noted for hosting the first annual White House Thanksgiving dinner.

***The Polks installed the first gas lights in the White House, replacing candles and oil lamps.***

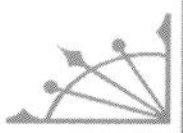

# Chocolate Caramel Fingers

*No cookie recipes can be traced directly to President and Mrs. Polk. However, the James K. Polk Memorial Auxiliary published* The James K. Polk Cookbook *to honor the First Family and to create an interest in their style of living and entertaining while in the White House. A delicious recipe from the cookbook is Chocolate Caramel Fingers, rich shortbread bars topped with a swirled buttery-brown sugar-chocolate mixture and lightly dusted with powdered sugar.*

2 CUPS PLAIN FLOUR
2 CUPS DARK BROWN SUGAR
1 CUP BUTTER (2 STICKS)
2 EGGS
1 TSP. SALT
2/3 TSP. BAKING SODA
1 TSP. BAKING POWDER
1 CUP SEMISWEET CHOCOLATE MORSELS
POWDERED SUGAR

1. Heat oven to 325°.
2. Melt butter in large saucepan and stir in sugar.
3. Add slightly beaten eggs.
4. Add sifted dry ingredients.
5. Stir in chocolate morsels last.
6. Pour batter into slightly greased and floured 12x17-inch roasting pan.
7. Bake for 20 to 25 minutes. Do not overcook. The top should appear glazed. The testing toothpick should be almost dry.
8. Remove from stove and brush immediately with powdered sugar.
9. Cool 15 minutes.
10. Cut into 1/2 x 3-inch strips (12 fingers pan-width and 5 pan-length)

YIELD: 60 FINGERS.

# Zachary Taylor (1784-1850)

## 12th President of the United States

(1849-1850)

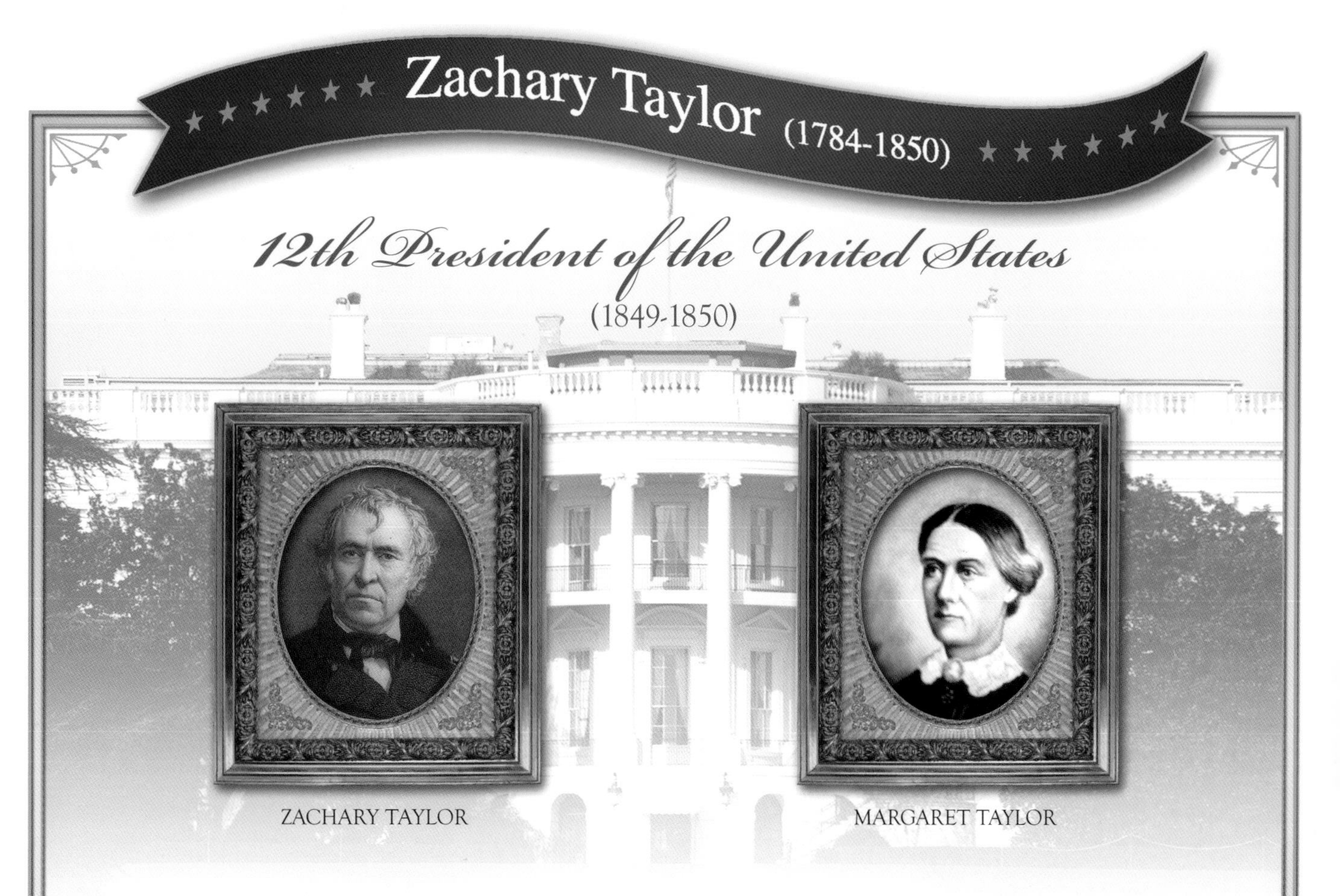

ZACHARY TAYLOR

MARGARET TAYLOR

President Zachary Taylor, nicknamed "Old Rough and Ready" for his years as a frontier general, served just over one year as President. His wife, First Lady Margaret, was in poor health and unable to perform her presidential entertaining duties. She kept her entertaining to family and friends who visited with her upstairs in the White House. Occasionally, First Lady Margaret would join her husband when he met with special groups. But usually, President Taylor's daughter, Betty Taylor Bliss, handled the hostess responsibilities.

Betty Bliss enjoyed giving elegant afternoon teas for Cabinet wives and Washington socialites—elegant affairs where waiters served from platters piled high with homemade "little cakes." A most likely "little cake" is the Kentucky Tea Cake. The recipe for these Kentucky Tea Cakes comes from Kentucky, where President Taylor spent his boyhood.

*As a soldier who never lived for very long in one location, President Taylor never had an official residence and never voted, not even in his own election. He finally cast his first ballot at age 62.*

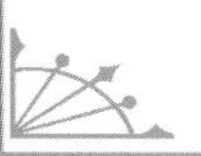



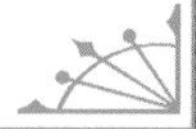

# Kentucky Tea Cakes

1/2 cup butter (1 stick)
1 1/2 cups sugar
3 eggs
4 Tbsp. white wine
Juice and rind of 1/2 lemon
Flour

1. Preheat oven to 400°.
2. In a large bowl, cream together butter and sugar.
3. In a small bowl, beat eggs until they are light and frothy.
4. Add beaten eggs to creamed mixture and mix well.
5. Add wine, lemon juice, and rind.
6. Add just enough flour to roll the dough evenly.
7. Cut the dough in rounds and place on a greased cookie sheet.
8. Bake 6 to 8 minutes until lightly browned.
9. Cool on rack.

Yield: 2 dozen tea cakes.

### PRESIDENT FOR A DAY

The Polk presidency ended at noon, March 4, 1849. President-elect Taylor refused to take the oath of office on that day because it was Sunday. Thus, there was no official President or Vice President from noon, March 4, until noon, March 5, when Taylor was sworn in. According to the law at the time, the President Pro Tempore of the Senate presided when there was no President or Vice President. On that Sunday, David Rice Atchison held that position. While Atchison was never sworn in, he was unofficially President for a day.

# Black Pepper Cookies

*Wait! Before you shriek at a cookie with black pepper and flip the page, give this recipe a chance. The bit of black pepper joined with the cinnamon and cloves adds a spicy punch to these brown sugar cookies. It's fun to reveal the "surprise" ingredient when everyone raves about them.*

2 EGGS, SEPARATED

1 CUP LIGHT BROWN SUGAR, PACKED

1 CUP FLOUR

1/4 TSP. SALT

1 TSP. CINNAMON

1/2 TSP. GROUND CLOVES

1/4 TSP. BLACK PEPPER

1/4 TSP. BAKING SODA

1/4 TSP. BAKING POWDER

1/2 CUP RAISINS

1/2 CUP CHOPPED NUTS

1. Preheat oven to 375°.
2. In a small bowl, beat 2 egg whites.
3. In another small bowl, beat 2 egg yolks.
4. Combine egg whites and yolks and mix.
5. Add brown sugar and mix again.
6. In another bowl, sift flour with salt, cinnamon, cloves, black pepper, baking soda, and baking powder.
7. Add the sifted ingredients to the eggs.
8. Stir in mixed raisins and nuts.
9. If dough is not stiff, add more flour. Blend well.
10. Drop by a tablespoon onto a greased baking sheet.
11. Bake for 5 to 7 minutes.
12. Cool on a rack.

YIELD: 5 DOZEN COOKIES.

## 13th President of the United States

(1850-1853)

MILLARD FILLMORE

ABIGAIL FILLMORE

The Fillmores are noted for numerous "firsts" for the White House. The first real bathtub with centrally heated running water was installed during the Fillmore administration. First Lady Abigail Fillmore, a former teacher, created the first library in the White House. Another first, unsettling to many people of that era, was the placement of the first iron cook stove in the White House. Even the White House chef disapproved and was aghast at the idea of cooking on such a "contraption." White House kitchen staff were skeptical about the merits of the new-fangled cook stove and refused to learn how to use it. In fact, the President himself had to study drawings at the United States Patent Office to learn how to operate the stove's drafts and pulleys. The following recipe for Charlottes was popular during Fillmore's youth.

# Charlottes

*This fruit-and-nut cookie surprises with its delicious sugar cookie taste and double-deluxe size. Even those reluctant to sample beyond today's chocolate chip cookie recipes find these early American cookies reminiscent of Grandma's best-loved cookie-jar cookies.*

1 cup butter (2 sticks)
1 cup light brown sugar, packed
1 cup sugar
2 eggs, beaten
3 cups flour
1 1/2 tsp. baking soda
1/2 tsp. salt
2 tsp. vanilla
1 cup chopped nuts, any variety
1 cup chopped dates
Granulated sugar for dipping

1. Preheat oven to 375°.
2. In a large bowl, cream butter and sugars thoroughly.
3. Beat in eggs.
4. In another bowl, sift flour, soda, and salt.
5. Add dry ingredients to creamed mixture and mix well.
6. Add vanilla.
7. Stir in dates and nuts. Blend with a strong wooden spoon.
8. Form into large balls about the size of a walnut.
9. Flatten balls with the bottom of a water glass dipped in flour.
10. Dip the top of each cookie in granulated sugar.
11. Bake cookies on a greased sheet about 3 inches apart for about 12 to 15 minutes.

Yield: 3 dozen Charlottes.

# Franklin Pierce (1804-1869)

## 14th President of the United States

(1853-1857)

FRANKLIN PIERCE

JANE PIERCE

*Pierce gave his 3,319-word inaugural address from memory—without the aid of notes.*

*While studying at Bowdoin College in Maine, Pierce had the lowest grades in his class. Fortunately, he improved his study habits and grraduated third in his class. Nathaniel Hawthorne and Henry Wadsworth Longfellow were fellow classmates.*

As natives of New Hampshire, President Franklin and First Lady Jane Pierce probably greatly enjoyed New Hampshire Seed Cookies, commonly baked during their childhood years. During the slave trades of the 18th century, plantation cooking introduced new flavors and spices, one being the benne (sesame) seed. The use of benne seeds became popular in South Carolina, and recipes using these flat seeds became common throughout the southern colonies. By the 19th century, the seed's popularity had expanded to New England.

# New Hampshire Seed Cookies

3/4 CUP BUTTER (1 1/2 STICKS)
1 1/2 CUPS LIGHT BROWN SUGAR, PACKED
2 EGGS
1 1/4 CUPS FLOUR
1/4 TSP. BAKING POWDER
1/2 CUP TOASTED SESAME SEEDS (TWO 1-OUNCE JARS)
1 TSP. VANILLA

1. Preheat oven to 375°.
2. Toast sesame seeds 3 to 5 minutes on an ungreased sheet until lightly browned. Watch so they do not burn.
3. In a small bowl, cream together softened butter and brown sugar.
4. Add eggs and mix well.
5. In a separate bowl, sift together flour and baking powder. Add toasted sesame seeds.
6. Stir dry ingredients carefully into the egg-butter mixture and mix well.
7. Add vanilla and mix again.
8. Drop by the teaspoon onto a greased cookie sheet.
9. Leave space for the cookies to spread.
10. Bake for 6 to 8 minutes until light brown.
11. Cool for a few minutes on the cookie sheet before removing to a rack to finish cooling.

YIELD: 3 TO 4 DOZEN COOKIES.

*Toasting the sesame seeds enhances the flavor of these cookies and gives them a crunchy texture.*

# James Buchanan (1791-1868)

## *15th President of the United States*

(1857-1861)

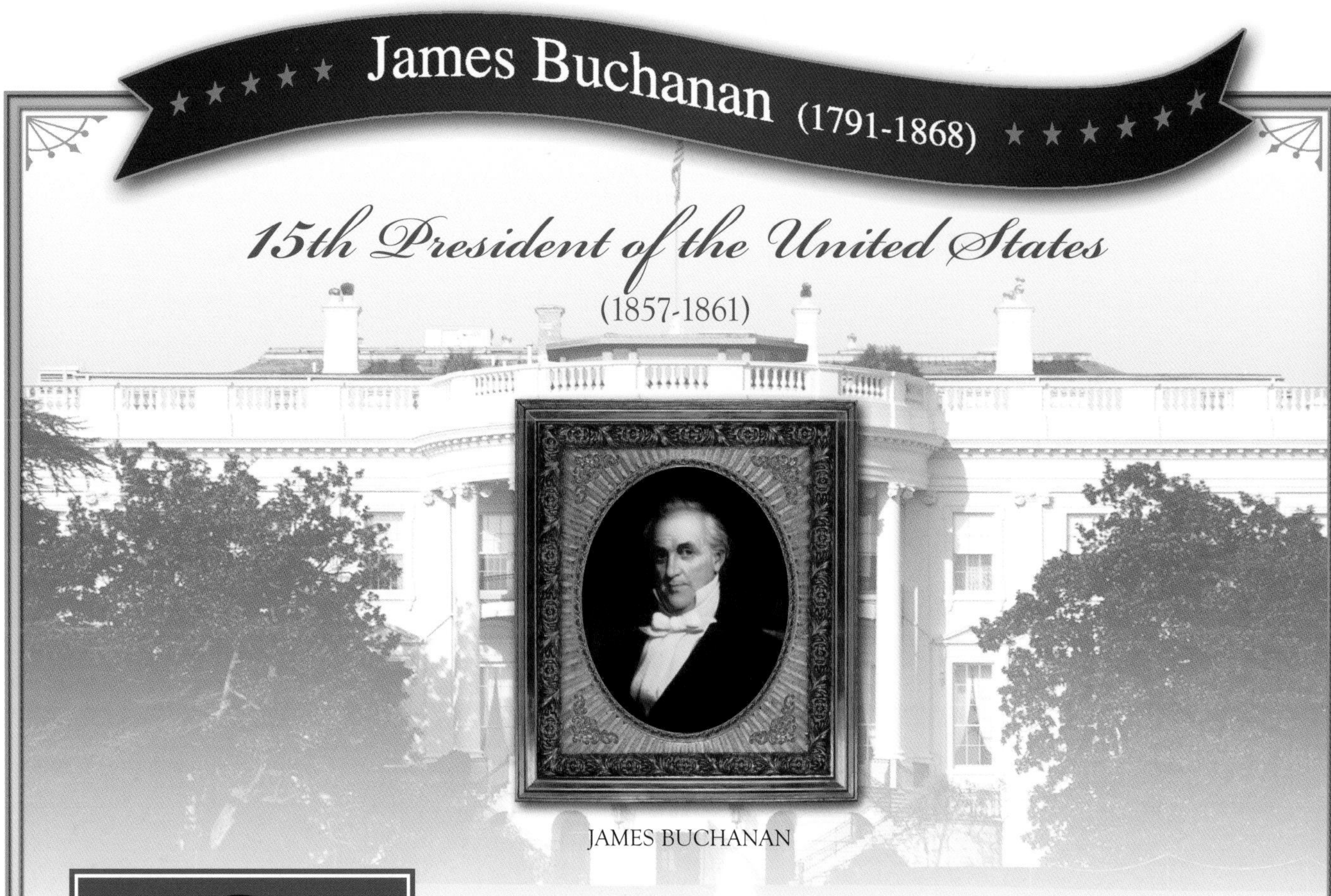

JAMES BUCHANAN

*Harriet Lane is called the "First Lady of the National Collection of Fine Arts" for donating to the government her sizable art collection, which is currently under the auspices of the Smithsonian Institution.*

President James Buchanan was the only President who never married. The White House hostess was his twenty-four-year-old niece, Harriet Lane. She brought gaiety to the weekly White House dinner parties. As political tensions increased among dignitaries and political adversaries, eventually leading to the Civil War, President Buchanan relied heavily on Ms. Lane's detailed planning. She worked out seating arrangements for White House dinners with special care and sensitivity to keep peace between the "Dixies," those guests from the South, and the "Yankee Doodles," the guests from the North.

President Buchanan and Ms. Lane are remembered for one of their last and most gracious acts: seeing that dinner was prepared and waiting for the incoming First Family, President and Mrs. Lincoln.

The recipe for German New Year's Cookies appeared in the 1861 cookbook, *Civil War Cooking: The Housekeeper's Encyclopedia*, by Mrs. E.F. Haskell. These cookies—which claim to keep for a year—were popular during Buchanan's presidency, as were Soft Cookies.

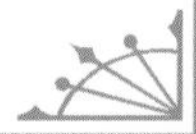

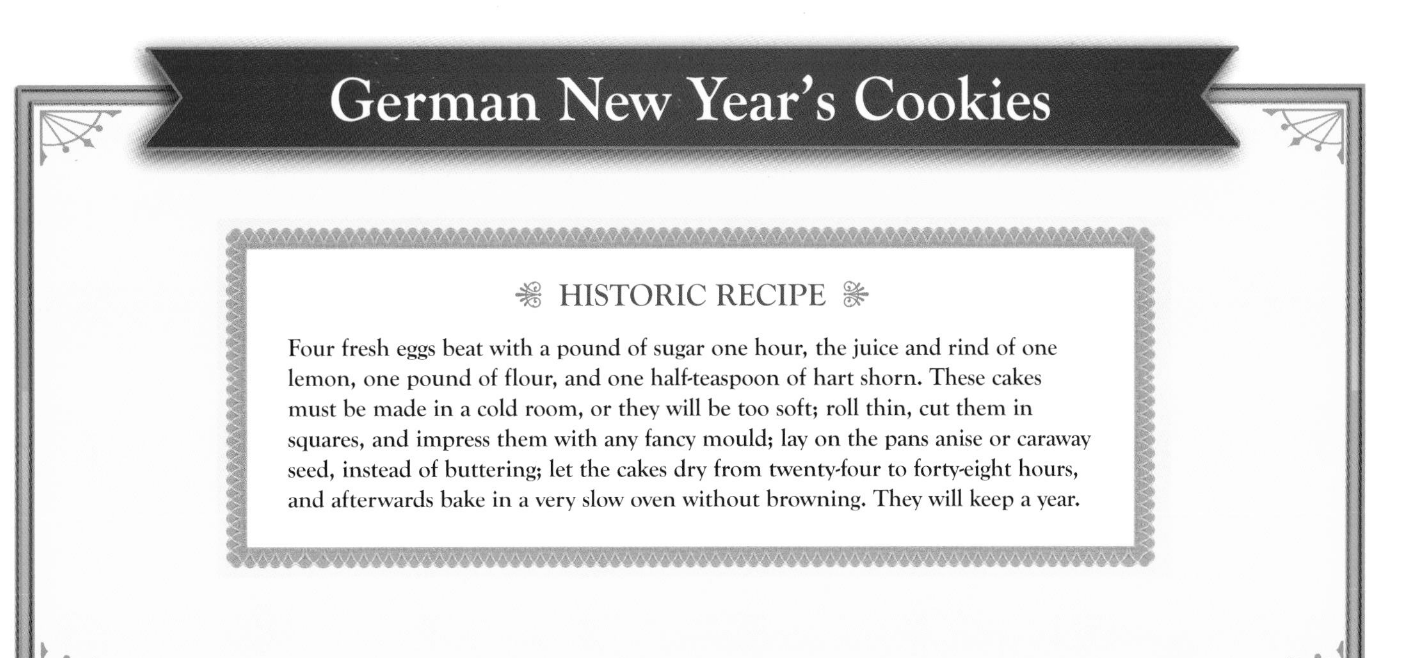

# German New Year's Cookies

HISTORIC RECIPE

Four fresh eggs beat with a pound of sugar one hour, the juice and rind of one lemon, one pound of flour, and one half-teaspoon of hart shorn. These cakes must be made in a cold room, or they will be too soft; roll thin, cut them in squares, and impress them with any fancy mould; lay on the pans anise or caraway seed, instead of buttering; let the cakes dry from twenty-four to forty-eight hours, and afterwards bake in a very slow oven without browning. They will keep a year.

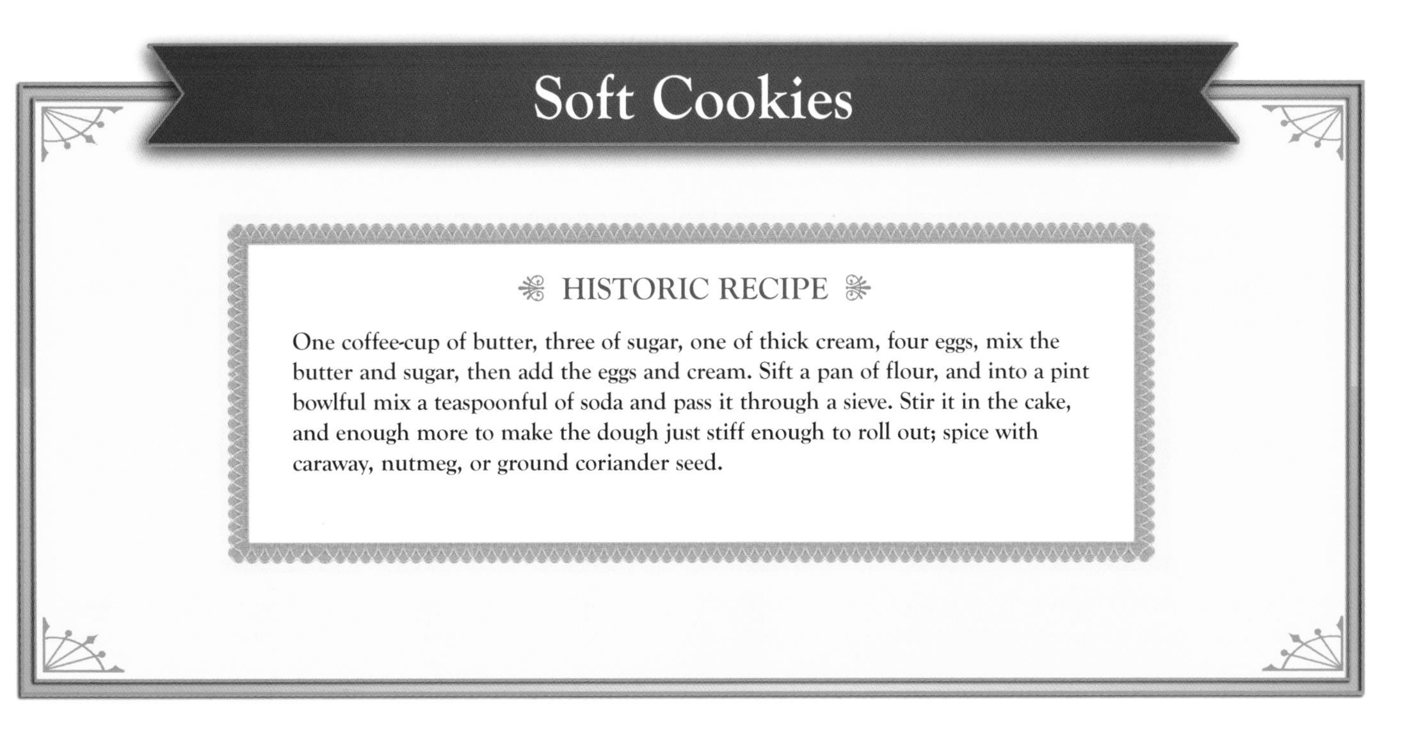

# Soft Cookies

HISTORIC RECIPE

One coffee-cup of butter, three of sugar, one of thick cream, four eggs, mix the butter and sugar, then add the eggs and cream. Sift a pan of flour, and into a pint bowlful mix a teaspoonful of soda and pass it through a sieve. Stir it in the cake, and enough more to make the dough just stiff enough to roll out; spice with caraway, nutmeg, or ground coriander seed.

# Apees

*As a boy, President Buchanan, along with most Pennsylvanians of that time, enjoyed Apees, delicious cookies probably named after Ann Page (A.P.), a famous 19th century cook from Philadelphia.*

3 CUPS FLOUR
1 1/2 TSP. BAKING SODA
1 1/2 CUPS LIGHT BROWN SUGAR, PACKED
1/4 TSP. CINNAMON
1/4 TSP. SALT
1/2 CUP SOFT BUTTER (1 STICK)
1/2 CUP MILK
1 TSP. VANILLA

1. Preheat oven to 350°.
2. In a large bowl, mix the flour, baking soda, brown sugar, cinnamon, and salt.
3. Add butter to the dry ingredients and mix well.
4. Add milk and vanilla to the mixture to make a soft dough.
5. Roll teaspoon of dough into a ball and press onto a cookie sheet into about 1/4-inch rounds.
6. Place rounds on an ungreased baking sheet.
7. Bake until edges are golden, 12 to 15 minutes.

YIELD: 3 TO 4 DOZEN APEES.

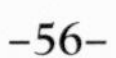

# Abraham Lincoln (1809-1865)

## 16th President of the United States

(1861-1865)

ABRAHAM LINCOLN

MARY LINCOLN

President Abraham Lincoln liked cakes and cookies that were heavily seasoned with ginger. Carl Sandburg, famous poet and biographer of Lincoln, recounts in his book, *Abraham Lincoln, The Prairie Years II*, the "gingerbread story" that Lincoln told in one of his debates with Stephen A. Douglas. The story is early evidence of Lincoln's compassionate spirit.

> "When we lived in Indiana," he said, "once in a while my mother used to get some sorghum and ginger and make some gingerbread. It wasn't often, and it was our biggest treat.
>
> One day I smelled the gingerbread and came into the house to get my share while it was still hot. My mother had baked me three gingerbread men. I took them out under a hickory tree to eat them.
>
> There was a family near us poorer than we were, and their boy came along as I sat down. 'Abe,' he said, 'gimme a man?' I gave him one. He crammed it into his mouth in two bites and looked at me while I was biting the legs off my first one. 'Abe,' he said, 'gimme that other'n.' I wanted it myself, but I gave it to him and as it followed the first I said to him,
>
> 'You seem to like gingerbread.'
>
> 'Abe,' he said 'I don't s'pose anybody on earth likes gingerbread better'n I do–and gets less'n I do.' "

# Gingerbread Men Cookies

*The recipe for the Gingerbread Men baked by President Lincoln's mother and so fondly remembered in his boyhood story was never preserved. Nor has any gingerbread recipe been found from his years in the White House. However, Lincoln did love gingerbread cookies, and could he have tasted the following recipe for Gingerbread Men cookies combining the spiciness of ginger, cinnamon, cloves, nutmeg and allspice with robust molasses–he would have given his presidential approval. Chill the dough for at least one hour before cutting out your favorite shapes.*

1/2 CUP BUTTER (1 STICK)
1/2 CUP SUGAR
1/2 CUP MOLASSES
1 EGG YOLK
2 CUPS SIFTED FLOUR
1/2 TSP. SALT
1/2 TSP. BAKING POWDER
1/2 TSP. BAKING SODA
1/2 TSP. CINNAMON
1 TSP. GROUND CLOVES
1 TSP. GINGER
1/2 TSP. NUTMEG
1/2 TSP. ALLSPICE

*On January 1, 1863, President Lincoln issued the Emancipation Proclamation, the document that led to the abolishment of slavery.*

*During the same year, President Lincoln also proclaimed Thanksgiving a national holiday, one devoted to gratitude and abundance.*

1. Preheat oven to 350°.
2. In a large bowl, cream the butter with the sugar until smooth.
3. Beat in the molasses and egg yolk.
4. In another bowl, sift together the flour, salt, baking powder, baking soda, and spices.
5. Gradually beat the flour mixture into the butter-egg mixture.

6. Cover and chill the dough for at least one hour.
7. On a lightly floured board, roll the dough to a 1/4-inch thickness.
8. Cut into gingerbread men or other desired shapes.
9. Place cookies about 2 inches apart on an ungreased cookie sheet.
10. Bake cookies for 8 to 10 minutes until firm.
11. Cool on the cookie sheet for a few minutes.
12. Remove cookies to a wire rack to cool thoroughly.
13. Decorate with Royal Icing, if desired.

YIELD: 3 DOZEN GINGERBREAD MEN COOKIES.

## Royal Icing

1 LARGE EGG WHITE
1 CUP POWDERED SUGAR
1/2 TSP. LEMON EXTRACT

1. In a large bowl, beat the egg white, powdered sugar, and lemon extract with an electric mixer for 6 to 8 minutes until icing is thick and holds it shape. If needed, add additional powdered sugar.
2. Using a pastry bag and decorator tube, outline the shape of each gingerbread man or create designs with the icing.
3. Allow the icing to dry before stacking cookies.
4. Store icing in a covered container in the refrigerator.

# Fruit Cookies

*The Lincoln family regularly purchased macaroon pyramids, cookies piled high and held together with spun or caramelized sugar. But Lincoln also enjoyed fruit, so along with macaroons, he kept his cupboard stocked with fruit cookies.*

1 1/2 cups sugar
1 cup soft butter (2 sticks)
3 well-beaten eggs
1 1/2 Tbsp. water
3 1/4 cups flour
1 tsp. baking soda
1/4 tsp. salt
1/2 tsp. cinnamon
1/2 cup currants
1/2 cup raisins, chopped
1 cup walnuts, chopped

1. Preheat oven to 350°.
2. In a large bowl, combine sugar with butter. Cream until fluffy.
3. Add eggs and water and beat thoroughly.
4. In another bowl, sift flour, soda, salt, and cinnamon.
5. Combine dry ingredients with butter and sugar mixture.
6. Add fruits and nuts and mix well.
7. Drop by teaspoon on a greased cookie sheet.
8. Bake for 15 minutes.
9. Remove to a rack to cool.

Yield: 4 dozen cookies.

# Andrew Johnson (1808-1875)

## 17th President of the United States

(1865-1869)

ANDREW JOHNSON

ELIZA JOHNSON

President Andrew and First Lady Eliza Johnson entertained with simple and gentle elegance. Their grown daughter, Martha Patterson, described her parents as "plain people from the mountains of Tennessee." Because of frailty and poor health, the First Lady was seldom seen at White House gatherings; instead, Martha stepped in to serve as hostess of the White House.

*During their young married years, Eliza Johnson taught her husband reading, writing, and arithmetic.*

The First Family totaled twelve, including the children and grandchildren. They enjoyed many family gatherings, such as popcorn parties and cozy evenings of roasting apples and chestnuts. The following adapted recipe comes from *The White House Cook Book,* 1887 Edition. Whether plain people or presidential people, the First Family no doubt enjoyed these Press Cookies popular in the late 19th century.

# Press Cookies

1 cup butter (2 sticks)
1 cup sugar
2 eggs
3 cups sifted flour
1 tsp. cinnamon or 1 tsp. grated lemon or orange rind
Colored sugar to decorate, if desired

1 Preheat oven to 375°.
2. Cream butter and sugar thoroughly.
3. Beat in eggs.
4. Add flour and cinnamon or lemon rind.
5. Stir dough until blended.
6. Press dough through a cookie press in a variety of shapes.
7. Sprinkle with colored sugar if desired.
8. Bake cookies on an ungreased cookie sheet for 10 to15 minutes.
9. Remove from sheet immediately.
10. Cool on a rack.

Yield: 7 dozen cookies.

# Ulysses S. Grant (1822-1885)

## *18th President of the United States*

(1869-1877)

ULYSSES S. GRANT　　JULIA GRANT

Even before President Ulysses S. Grant entered the White House in 1869, he had become a celebrity as a successful general. First Lady Julia Grant described the presidential years as "the happiest period" of her life. The President and First Lady entertained extensively and lavishly with formal dinners, their weekly state dinners consisting of as many as 29 courses and 6 types of wine. In between courses, guests would walk around the White House grounds and enjoy a Roman punch, the then-popular sorbet-type drink. After the short break, everyone would return to resume the extravagant feast.

A newspaper correspondent at the time described the dessert courses at one such dinner: "The dessert is inaugurated by the destruction of a rice pudding, it is such a pudding as would make our grandmothers clap their hands with joy. After the rice pudding, canned peaches, pears and quinces are served. Then follow confectionary, nuts, ice cream, coffee and chocolate . . . ."

Unlike the dinner parties of other Presidents, no entertainment followed these elaborate feasts. Instead, guests would chat for only about 15 minutes in the Blue or Red Room. The Grants would then bid all good night and retire for the evening, leaving their guests—no doubt with very full stomachs—to do the same.

Devoted parents, the President and First Lady turned their family meals into play time. President Grant would shape his dinner rolls into little balls and toss them toward his children. If someone got hit, he would immediately apologize with a gentle kiss—which, of course, was the point.

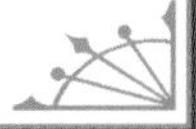

# Lemon Cookies

*This recipe for Lemon Cookies appeared in* The White House Cook Book, *1887 Edition, as a presidential favorite and may have been affectionately baked for the Grant children. A Lemon Drops recipe that follows is a modern adaptation.*

### HISTORIC RECIPE

Four cups of sifted flour, or enough for a stiff dough; one teacupful of butter, two cups of sugar, the juice of one lemon, and the grated peel from the outside, three eggs, whipped very light. Beat thoroughly each ingredient, adding after all is in a half teaspoonful of soda, dissolved in a tablespoonful of milk. Roll out as any cookies, and bake a light brown. Use no other wetting.

# Lemon Drops

1/2 cup butter (1 stick)
1/2 cup margarine (1 stick)
1/2 cup sugar
1/2 cup brown sugar, packed
1 egg
1 Tbsp. lemon juice
1 tsp. finely grated lemon rind
2 1/2 cups flour
1/4 tsp. baking soda
1 tsp. salt
Powdered sugar

1. Preheat oven to 375°.
2. In a large bowl, cream butter, margarine, and sugars.
3. Add egg, lemon juice, and lemon rind, mixing well.
4. In a separate small bowl, sift flour, baking soda, and salt together.
5. Add half of the flour mixture to the butter mixture and beat until smooth. Add remaining flour and mix well.
6. Drop by teaspoon onto an ungreased cookie sheet.
7. Bake 10 to 12 minutes.
8. Remove cookies to a rack and cool thoroughly.
9. Dust with powdered sugar.

Yield: 3 dozen Lemon Drops.

# Rutherford B. Hayes (1822-1893)

## *19th President of the United States*

(1877-1881)

RUTHERFORD B. HAYES

LUCY HAYES

*In 1877, President Hayes first used a telephone when he spoke to Alexander Graham Bell, inventor of the telephone. Two years later, President Hayes installed the first telephone in the White House. The phone number was simply the number "1".*

Although President Rutherford and First Lady Lucy Hayes entertained guests with formal parties, both preferred dining with close friends. They loved living in the White House and turned the sprawling mansion into a comfortable home for themselves and their children. First Lady Lucy was unkindly nicknamed "Lemonade Lucy" by some in Washington, for she refused to serve alcohol in the White House, instead supplying reception guests with lemonade, tea, coffee, water, and other refreshments.

Despite her nickname, First Lady Lucy was so greatly admired and popular with fellow Americans that three famous poets of the time, Oliver Wendell Holmes, John G. Whittier, and Henry Wadsworth Longfellow, honored her in their poetry.

# Hermits

*The recipe for Hermits is taken from* Miss Parloa's New Cook Book, *published in 1882. This cookbook was part of First Lady Lucy Hayes's personal collection of books. A modern adaptation follows.*

### HISTORIC RECIPE

Two cupfuls of sugar, one of butter, one of raisins (stoned and chopped), three eggs, half a teaspoonful of soda, dissolved in three tablespoonfuls of milk; a nutmeg, one teaspoonful each of clove and cinnamon, and six cupfuls of flour. Roll about one-fourth of an inch thick, and cut with a round cake cutter. Bake in a rather quick oven. It will take about twelve minutes.

1 cup butter (2 sticks)
2 cups light brown sugar, packed
2 eggs
3 1/2 cups flour
1 tsp. baking powder
1/2 tsp. salt
1 tsp. baking soda
2 tsp. cinnamon
1 tsp. nutmeg
1/2 cup sour cream or buttermilk
1 cup chopped walnuts
2 cups raisins
1 cup dates
Whole walnut halves, as garnish

1. Preheat oven to 350°.
2. In a large bowl, blend together butter and brown sugar.
3. Beat in eggs.
4. Stir in flour, baking powder, salt, and soda.
5. Add spices.
6. Stir in sour cream or buttermilk.
7. Add walnuts, raisins, and dates.
8. Stir well.
9. Drop by teaspoon onto a greased baking sheet.
10. Top each cookie with a whole walnut half.
11. Bake for 12 to15 minutes.
12. Remove to a wire rack to cool.

Yield: 6 dozen Hermits.

*It is believed that the title "First Lady" first appeared in an 1877 newspaper article referring to Lucy Hayes during her husband's inauguration. The title gained popularity in 1911 in a comedy about Dolley Madison, entitled* The First Lady in the Land.

# Lady's-Fingers

*This recipe for Lady's-Fingers comes from another cookbook in Lucy Hayes's personal library. In* Practical Cooking, and Dinner Giving, *the First Lady inscribed in her own handwriting: "Mrs. R.B. Hayes, Fremont, Ohio, 2 Aug 1881." Fremont, Ohio, is the location of the Hayes home, Spiegel Grove, and of the presidential library.*

## HISTORIC RECIPE

Mix six yolks of eggs with half a pound of powdered sugar; work the preparation with a spoon until it is frothy; then mix into it the whites of six eggs well beaten, and at the same time a quarter of a pound of flour, dried and sifted. Put this batter into a meringue bag, and squeeze it through in strips, two or three inches long, and sprinkle over some fine sugar; bake in a slack oven twelve or fourteen minutes.

Lucy Hayes in White House Conservatory with Carrie Davis (daughter of artist Theodore Davis, who created the Hayes White House China), Scott Hayes, and Fanny Hayes.

# Lady's-Fingers

*The following is an updated recipe for Lady's-Fingers.*

4 egg whites
4 egg yolks
2/3 cup white sugar
3/4 cup flour
Pinch of salt
1/2 tsp. baking powder
1 tsp. vanilla
Powdered sugar

1. Preheat oven to 400°.
2. Line two cookie sheets with parchment paper.
3. In a large mixing bowl, beat egg whites and 2 tablespoons of the sugar with an electric mixer on medium-high speed until whites are stiff and glossy.
4. In another bowl, beat the egg yolks and remaining sugar with an electric mixer set on medium for about 3 minutes, until the mixture is pale yellow and thick.
5. Sift the flour with the baking powder and salt.
6. Fold half of the egg whites into the yolk mixture.
7. Add flour mixture and then remaining egg whites and vanilla.
8. Fold to mix thoroughly so the mixture is smooth.
9. Fit a large pastry bag with a 3/4-inch plain or fluted decorator tip.
10. Fill the bag with the mixture.
11. Pipe fingers about 4 1/2 inches long onto the baking sheet.
12. Dust the Lady's-Fingers with powdered sugar.
13. Bake for about 6 to 8 minutes or until just firm and very light brown on the outside and soft in the center.
14. Cool on parchment paper for a few minutes, lifting each Lady's-Finger with a spatula to avoid sticking.

Yield: 5 dozen Lady's-Fingers.

These light Lady's-Fingers are an elegant complement to fresh fruit. They can also be used in preparing other desserts that call for ladyfingers.

# The United States White House Easter Egg Roll

Easter Egg Roll during Grover Cleveland's presidency
*Frank Leslie's Illustrated Weekly*, April 23, 1887

Many believe that President James and First Lady Dolley Madison initiated the White House Easter Egg Roll, now a yearly tradition. The festive race originally took place on the lawn of the United States Capitol. An old description penned by an unknown author of one of those early celebrations reads:

> At first the children sit sedately in long rows; each has brought a basket of gay-colored hard-boiled eggs, and those on the upper terrace send them rolling to the line next below, and those pass on the ribbon-like streams to hundreds at the foot, who scramble for the hopping eggs and hurry panting to the top to start them down again. And as the sport warms, those on top who have rolled all the eggs they brought finally roll themselves, shrieking with laughter. Now comes a swirl of

> curls, ribbons and furbelows [ruffles], somebody's dainty maid indifferent to the bumps and grass stains. A set of boys who started in a line of six with joined hands [is] trying to come down in somersaults without breaking the chain.

When the Easter Egg Roll was stopped because of damage to the Capitol grounds, President Rutherford and First Lady Lucy Hayes sympathetically reinstated the tradition in 1878. They invited Washington children to use the White House lawn instead. The annual event was discontinued again during both World War I and World War II and also during the reconstruction era of President Truman. It was President Dwight and First Lady Mamie Eisenhower who resumed the festive ritual at the White House. Today, thanks to the Hayes family, the White House Easter Egg Roll, celebrated on Easter Monday, continues on the South Lawn.

# James A. Garfield (1831-1881)

## 20th President of the United States

(1881)

JAMES GARFIELD

LUCRETIA GARFIELD

Upon taking the oath of office, President Garfield turned and kissed his wife and his mother—the first public show of affection by a President.

First Lady Lucretia was the first presidential wife to plan refurnishing the White House with authentic pieces. She spent most of her spare time in the Library of Congress, researching White House history and the mansion's contents.

President James and First Lady Lucretia Garfield brought their cheerful family to the White House in 1881. During the brief administration of less than one year, they hosted White House dinners and twice-weekly receptions. While these events were enjoyable, the Garfields preferred literary circles or informal parties.

# Crisp Cookies

*This recipe for Crisp Cookies appeared in* The White House Cook Book, *1887 Edition. A typical cookie recipe of this era, the Crisp Cookie has a delicate dusting of sprinkled sugar.*

## HISTORIC RECIPE

One cup of butter, two cups of sugar, three eggs well beaten, a teaspoonful of soda and two of cream of tartar, a spoonful of milk, one teaspoonful of nutmeg and one of cinnamon, flour enough to make a soft dough just stiff enough to roll out. Try a pint of sifted flour to begin with, working it in gradually. Spread a little sweet milk over each, and sprinkle with sugar. Bake in a quick oven a light brown.

*James Garfield could write Latin with one hand and Greek with the other at the same time.*

*He was the first President to campaign in two languages, English and German.*

*On Election Day, November 2, 1880, Garfield was at the same time a member of the House, a Senator-elect, and the President-elect.*

# Crisp Cookies

*The following adaptation of Crisp Cookies combines ingredients from the 19th century recipe with two favorite tastes from the 20th century–vanilla and chocolate.*

1/3 cup butter (5 1/2 Tbsp.)
2/3 cup semisweet chocolate chips
1/2 cup sugar
1 egg
1/2 cup flour
1/8 tsp. salt
1 tsp. vanilla
1/3 cup chopped nuts
1/3 cup semisweet chocolate chips

1. Preheat oven to 400°.
2. Combine butter and 2/3 cup chocolate chips. Heat in the microwave oven until melted, checking every 30 seconds. Stir to blend.
3. Stir in sugar.
4. Add the egg and beat well. Stir in flour, salt, and vanilla.
5. Spread batter into a well-greased 15 x 10 x 1-inch baking pan.
6. Sprinkle nuts and remaining chocolate chips over the top.
7. Bake for 12 minutes.
8. Cut into squares immediately.

Yield: 3 dozen Crisp Cookies.

# Chester A. Arthur (1829-1886)

## 21st President of the United States

(1881-1885)

CHESTER A. ARTHUR

President Chester A. Arthur took an active role in White House entertaining. Because he was a widower, his sister, Mary McElroy, served as hostess at White House gatherings. President Arthur, however, planned the White House dinners himself, giving his guests formal and lavish feasts. He presented bouquets of roses to the women and boutonnieres to the men. At receptions, he served little cakes, called Rocks, with afternoon tea.

The recipe for Rocks dates back centuries to England, maybe even to the days of King Arthur. To get a taste of a President Arthur reception and his penchant for luxurious living, try this indulgence: brew a cup of your favorite tea, arrange some chunky Rocks on your most elegant china plate, and place both tea and cookies next to a small vase of lovely flowers. Sip, sample, and simply enjoy.

*President Arthur sold twenty-four wagonloads of old White House items he considered "junk." Some objects sold included children belongings from the Grant and Hayes families and Abe Lincoln's trousers and silk hat.*

# Rocks

2/3 cup butter (1 stick + 5 1/3 Tbsp.)
1 cup light brown sugar, packed
2 eggs
2 cups flour
1/2 tsp. ground cloves
1 1/2 tsp. cinnamon
1 tsp. baking powder
1 1/4 Tbsp. hot water
1 cup chopped nuts, any variety
1 cup raisins
1 cup dates

*In 1881, for the second time in American history, there were three Presidents in one year: Hayes, Garfield, and Arthur.*

1. Preheat oven to 375°.
2. In a large bowl, cream butter with sugar and eggs until fluffy.
3. In separate bowl, sift flour with cloves and cinnamon.
4. Beat the flour into the butter-egg mixture.
5. Dissolve baking powder in hot water. Add to the dough. Mix well.
6. Blend in nuts, raisins, and dates. Mix well.
7. Drop by teaspoon onto a greased baking sheet.
8. Bake about 10 to 12 minutes.
9. Cool on a rack.

Yield: 4 dozen Rocks.

# Grover Cleveland (1837-1908)

## 22nd President of the United States

(1885-1889)

GROVER CLEVELAND

FRANCES CLEVELAND

In 1885 President Grover Cleveland entered the White House a bachelor. A year later, at the age of 49, he married Frances Folsom, becoming the only President to be married in the White House. Frances was just twenty-one-years old and the youngest First Lady. The President and First Lady continued the traditional New Year's Day and Fourth of July receptions. To accommodate the women who worked all week in Washington offices, Mrs. Cleveland scheduled an extra reception on Saturdays so that they too could attend and enjoy her hospitality. The popularity of these receptions grew rapidly until at one reception more than nine thousand guests passed through the Blue Room to shake hands with the First Lady.

The Clevelands were fond of simple American food: chops, steaks, corned beef and cabbage, and plain frosted cake. This traditional American recipe for Snickerdoodles was a great favorite in the White House after a hearty meal—but not just in the White House. Across the nation's kitchens, the cookies melted into eager mouths, although often called by other names: Graham Jakes, Brambles, Tangle Breeches, and Kinkawoodles. But a Snickerdoodle by any other name remains as tasty.

This drawing, *The President's Wedding,* illustrates the marriage of Grover Cleveland and Frances Folsom.

***Although many people think the Baby Ruth candy bar got its name from the baseball player, the Curtiss Candy Company claimed it was named after the President and First Lady Cleveland's baby daughter, Ruth. The company promoted the candy bar by hiring World War I pilots to barnstorm cities and small towns. They dropped thousands of Baby Ruth bars by parachute from their biplanes.***

# Snickerdoodles

*When preparing this recipe, allow about two hours to chill the dough before forming and baking the cookies.*

2 EGGS
1 1/2 CUPS SUGAR
1 CUP BUTTER SOFTENED (2 STICKS)
1 TSP. VANILLA
2 3/4 CUPS FLOUR
1/2 TSP. SALT
1 TSP. BAKING SODA
2 TSP. CINNAMON
2 TBSP. SUGAR

1. Preheat oven to 400°.
2. In large bowl, beat eggs and gradually add sugar.
3. Stir in butter and mix well.
4. Add vanilla.
5. In a smaller bowl, sift flour with salt and baking soda.
6. Add sifted flour, salt, and baking soda to the egg mixture and mix thoroughly.
7. Chill dough for about two hours.
8. In a small bowl, mix cinnamon with sugar.
9. Form cookie dough into 1-inch balls.
10. Roll balls into cinnamon and sugar mixture.
11. Place coated balls on ungreased cookie sheet.
12. Bake 8 to 10 minutes or until light brown.

YIELD: 3 TO 4 DOZEN SNICKERDOODLES.

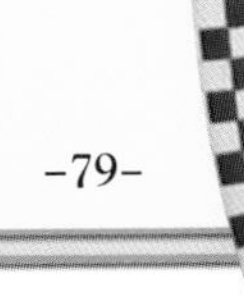

> *In 1891, President and First Lady Harrison installed electricity throughout the Executive Mansion, replacing gas lights.*

Happiest when surrounded by noisy children, close friends, and extended family, President Benjamin and First Lady Caroline Harrison looked for occasions to hold a family gathering. One such occasion took place in December 1889. The First Family put the first Christmas tree inside the White House, knowing that where there is a Christmas tree, family is sure to gather. Like most American families, the Harrisons enjoyed the holiday with loved ones, taking pleasure in the abundance of delicious desserts. A festive Harrison Christmas dinner was usually topped off with mince pie, American plum pudding, tutti fruitti ice cream, ladyfingers, Carlsbad wafers, and macaroons, followed by fruit and coffee.

# Chocolate Macaroons

*This chocolate macaroon recipe from* The White House Cook Book, *1887 Edition, was popular during the era of President Harrison and may have been baked during his Christmas celebrations.*

### HISTORIC RECIPE

Put three ounces of plain chocolate in a pan and melt on a slow fire; then work it to a thick paste with one pound of powdered sugar and the whites of three eggs; roll the mixture down to the thickness of about one-quarter of an inch; cut it in small, round pieces with a paste cutter, either plain or scalloped; butter a pan slightly and dust it with flour and sugar in equal quantities; place in the pan the pieces of mixture and bake in a hot but not too quick oven.

*The following recipe is a modern adaptation of chocolate macaroons.*

2 EGG WHITES
1/4 TSP. SALT
1/2 CUP SUGAR
1/2 TSP. VANILLA
ONE 8-OUNCE PACKAGE SEMISWEET CHOCOLATE CHIPS, MELTED
1 1/2 CUPS MOIST, SHREDDED COCONUT

1. Preheat oven to 300°.
2. Beat egg whites with electric beater until soft peaks form.
3. Continue beating, gradually adding sugar until stiff peaks form.
4. Fold in vanilla and salt.
5. Fold in melted chocolate chips and coconut.
6. Drop mixture by teaspoon 2 inches apart on cookie sheets lined with parchment paper.
7. Bake for about 20 minutes or until tops are set.
8. Cool slightly before removing to a wire rack to cool completely.

YIELD: 2 TO 3 DOZEN MACAROONS.

# Two Way Cookies

*Elizabeth S. Walker, the wife of Benjamin Harrison's grandson, contributed the following recipe to* The President Harrison Home Recipes *cookbook. Called Two Way Cookies, this one recipe creates two types of cookies.*

1 CUP BUTTER (2 STICKS)
1 CUP SUGAR
2 EGGS, SEPARATED
1 TSP. VANILLA
2 CUPS FLOUR
1 CUP CHOPPED WALNUTS
JELLY OR PRESERVES OF YOUR CHOICE
MINI CHOCOLATE CHIPS

**CAROLINE HARRISON**
**— started the White House china collection when she found china from previous administrations stored in the White House.**

1. Preheat oven to 350°.
2. In a bowl, beat butter and sugar until fluffy.
3. Beat in egg yolks and vanilla.
4. Mix in flour until well blended.
5. In a separate small bowl, slightly beat egg whites with fork.
6. Shape half of dough into 1-inch balls.
7. Dip balls into beaten egg whites and roll them in the nuts.
8. Make a thumbprint in the middle of each ball and fill with jelly.
9. Shape the other half of the dough into balls.
10. Flatten balls slightly (do not dip in egg whites).
11. Press mini chocolate chips into cookies.
12. Bake 20 minutes.

YIELD: 2 DOZEN COOKIES ONE WAY, 2 DOZEN THE OTHER WAY.

# Grover Cleveland (1837-1908)

## *24th President of the United States*

(1893-1897)

GROVER CLEVELAND

FRANCES CLEVELAND

Grover Cleveland served two nonconsecutive terms as the 22nd and 24th President of the United States. See Grover Cleveland, 22nd President, to learn about his presidency and to try the recipe for Snickerdoodles.

# William McKinley (1843-1901)

## 25th President of the United States

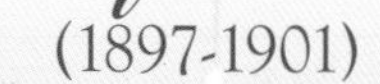

(1897-1901)

WILLIAM MCKINLEY

IDA MCKINLEY

**Refrigerators hadn't been invented yet during McKinley's time, so perishables such as meats, fruits, and vegetables were kept cool in a wooden cabinet filled with a block of ice, the "icebox."**
**In addition to preparing and cooking all those dishes for the McKinleys, kitchen staff lifted and hauled blocks of ice to the icebox to keep food cold. The icebox had been in use at the White House since the Polk administration. Not until 1926, during the Calvin Coolidge presidency, was the first refrigerator put into the White House.**

The administration of President William and First Lady Ida McKinley flourished at the height of the Victorian era and enjoyed Victorian extravagance and opulence in entertaining. The First Family set the record for abundant fare by serving a staggering 71 courses at one of their formal White House dinners.

Would you rather *eat* 71 courses, cleaning your plate after each one—so as not to offend the host, of course—or would you rather *prepare* 71 courses, peeling, cleaning, dicing, slicing, seasoning, simmering, and stewing, not to mention washing the pots and pans? As for me, I think I'd rather eat.

# Icebox Cookies

*Popular Icebox Cookies took their name from cookie dough chilled in the icebox. We now chill dough in our modern refrigerator before slicing and baking. Allow some time to prepare these cookies since the dough must be refrigerated overnight or for at least four hours.*

1 CUP SOFT BUTTER (2 STICKS)
1 CUP LIGHT BROWN SUGAR, PACKED
2 EGGS, WELL BEATEN
1 1/2 TSP. VANILLA
1 TSP. SALT
3 CUPS FLOUR
1/2 TSP. BAKING SODA
1/2 CUP FINELY CHOPPED NUTS, ANY VARIETY

1. Preheat oven to 400°.
2. In a large bowl, cream butter and brown sugar.
3. Add well-beaten eggs and mix well.
4. In a smaller bowl, sift flour with baking soda and salt.
5. Add flour mixture to the egg-butter mixture.
6. Beat well and then add nuts.
7. Divide the dough into 2 or 3 portions.
8. Place each portion on a piece of plastic wrap and shape the dough into a roll about 2 inches in diameter.
9. Wrap rolls tightly and refrigerate overnight or for at least 4 hours.
10. Slice 1/8 to 1/4 inch thick and place on an ungreased cookie sheet.
11. Bake 7 to 9 minutes.
12. Remove immediately to a rack to cool.

YIELD: 6 TO 7 DOZEN COOKIES.

# Theodore Roosevelt (1858-1919)

## 26th President of the United States

(1901-1909)

THEODORE ROOSEVELT

EDITH ROOSEVELT

President Roosevelt was the first President to

- — ride in an automobile.
- — fly in an airplane.
- — visit a foreign country, Panama, while in office.
- — receive the Nobel Peace Prize.

President Theodore and First Lady Edith Roosevelt had a sweet tooth each, especially for buttery, sugary cookies. Many a peeking White House eye caught the President gobbling cookies as fast as they appeared on the plate. This recipe for Sand Tarts is written on the inside cover of one of Edith Roosevelt's many cookbooks. The family offered these cookies with coffee to friends who dropped in on Christmas morning at their family home, Sagamore Hill. Cookies in the morning? To a sweet tooth, any time of day is cookie time.

# Sagamore Hill Sand Tarts

1 cup butter (2 sticks)
2 cups sugar
2 eggs + 1 egg separated
4 cups flour
2 tsp. vanilla
Sugar and cinnamon

1. Preheat oven to 350°.
2. Cream butter until smooth.
3. Add sugar and mix until light and fluffy.
4. Add 2 eggs, one by one, beating after each addition.
5. Beat in one additional egg yolk and vanilla.
6. Stir in sifted flour. Mix again well.
7. Roll the dough on a lightly floured board, about 1/8-inch thick.
8. Cut with a 2 1/2-inch cookie cutter, any shape.
9. In small bowl, beat remaining egg white with a fork just enough to stir it up a bit.
10. Brush the egg white on top of the cookies.
11. Sprinkle with a cinnamon-sugar mixture and bake on a greased cookie sheet for about 8 minutes.

Yield: 6 dozen tarts.

For a holiday variation, eliminate the extra egg white and cinnamon-sugar topping. Use Christmas cookie cutters. Bake as you would regular sand tarts. When the cookies are cool, ice them or sprinkle them with sugar in Christmas colors.

This 1903 photo shows the President, his wife Edith, and their six children at the family home of Sagamore Hill at Oyster Bay on Long Island, New York. President Roosevelt loved his family and spent many hours with his children enjoying outdoor adventures such as hiking and rowing. (Children from the left: Quentin, Teddy Jr., Archie, Alice, Kermit, and Ethel)

*The Roosevelt children had many pets, including dogs, cats, rabbits, a flying squirrel, a badger, a kangaroo rat, and a small black bear. At the White House, they also had a pony, named Algonquin. When one of the children, Archie, took to bed sick, the other children smuggled Algonquin into the White House elevator and then up to Archie's room to cheer him up.*

# "Princess" Alice's Jumbles

Teenagers have a knack for turning a house upside down. Alice Roosevelt, the President's oldest child, was a spirited teenager with a style very much her own. She often wore riding breeches instead of dresses and kept a pet snake named Emily Spinach. Revealing his frustration with his teenage daughter, President Roosevelt said, "I can do one of two things. I can be the President of the United States, or I can control Alice. I cannot possibly do both."

The particulars of her flamboyant social life as a debutante spread beyond the White House, captivating public and news media attention. In a fifteen-month period, she attended 407 dinners, 350 balls, and 300 parties. The press soon designated her "Princess Alice." These ring-shaped Jumbles were said to be one of her favorite cookies. Rich and delicate, they are indeed fit for a princess.

2 cups sugar
1 cup butter (2 sticks)
3 eggs, well beaten
1 tsp. baking powder
1/2 cup milk
Flour

*First Lady Edith Roosevelt initiated the White House display of portraits of the First Ladies.*

1. Preheat oven to 350°.
2. Cream sugar with butter until light and fluffy.
3. Add well-beaten eggs, baking powder, milk, and just enough flour to form a soft dough. Mix well.
4. Roll dough into a very thin sheet on a floured board.
5. Cut into rings with a doughnut cutter.
6. Bake about 5 minutes, only until lightly browned.

Yield: 4 dozen jumbles.

# Rich Man's Shortbread

*Another favorite cookie of the Roosevelt family was Rich Man's Shortbread, a delicious bar topped with a toffee mixture and glazed with chocolate.*

## Shortbread

1/2 cup unsalted butter, softened (1 stick)
1 1/3 cups all purpose flour
4 1/2 Tbsp. superfine sugar

## Toffee Topping

1/2 cup unsalted butter (1 stick)
4 1/2 Tbsp. superfine sugar
2 Tbsp. corn syrup
1/4 tsp. vanilla
2/3 cup sweetened condensed milk (do not use evaporated milk)

## Chocolate Glaze

7 ounces semisweet chocolate

### To make shortbread:

1. Preheat oven to 350°.
2. In small mixer bowl, cream butter and sugar with an electric mixer at medium speed until light and fluffy.
3. Stir in flour with wooden spoon.
4. Press into 10 x 6-inch baking dish.
5. Bake for 20 to 25 minutes until golden brown.
6. Cool the pan on a rack.

### To make toffee topping:

1. In heavy medium saucepan, combine butter, sugar, corn syrup, and condensed milk.
2. Bring to boil over medium-high heat, stirring constantly.

3. Boil for 5 minutes, stirring constantly.
4. Stir in vanilla.
5. Quickly pour over cooled shortbread, spreading evenly.
6. Cool topped shortbread on rack at least 1 hour.

**To make chocolate glaze:**

1. In the top of a double boiler, melt chocolate.
2. Pour over cooled toffee topping, spreading evenly.
3. Cool on rack until set.
4. Cut into bars.

YIELD: 3 DOZEN BARS.

# William H. Taft (1857-1930)

## 27th President of the United States

(1909-1913)

WILLIAM TAFT

HELEN "NELLIE" TAFT

> *Nellie Taft was responsible for planting 3,000 cherry trees donated by the City of Tokyo in Washington, D.C.*

President William and First Lady Helen Taft, affectionately known as Nellie, invited guests to dine with them almost every day—and not just at dinner, but at almost every meal. President Taft was known for his love of food, and lots of it, as evidenced by his weight of more than three hundred pounds.

The First Family spent their summers in Beverly, Massachusetts. While Taft ate his share of cookies, neither the Beverly Historical Society and Museum nor the William Howard Taft Historical Site has records of favorite cookie recipes. However, from nearby Marblehead, Massachusetts, comes a post-Revolutionary War tall tale about the creation of Joe Frogger cookies. If President Taft was not aware of this folklore, he would have enjoyed it, and he definitely would have devoured the cookies, given his gourmand tastes.

# Joe Frogger Cookies

*The* Marblehead Magazine *provided the following history of the Joe Frogger cookie.*

Named for Revolutionary War patriot, Joseph Brown, these large cookies were said to be the size of the frogs in Black Joe's Pond. Marblehead's early fishermen used to take the cookies with them on long voyages to the Grand Banks as a standard part of the ship's provisions. The ingredients of rum and seawater acted as preservatives. They are now a cherished Marblehead tradition with original recipes circulating rapidly for historic authentication by native Marbleheaders. Lucretia Brown, Joseph's wife, first made these cookies in the 1800s. While today the cookies are mostly round, in the beginning they were described as lily-pad shaped.

More information on Black Joe and Lucretia Brown and their life on Gingerbread Hill can be found on the *Marblehead Magazine* website.

7 CUPS FLOUR
1 TBSP. SALT
1 TBSP. FRESH GINGER
1 TSP. EACH CLOVE, FRESH NUTMEG, ALLSPICE
3/4 CUP HOT WATER
1/4 CUP RUM
2 TSP. BAKING SODA
2 CUPS VERY DARK MOLASSES
1 CUP SHORTENING
2 CUPS SUGAR

1. Preheat oven to 375°.
2. In a bowl, sift flour, salt, ginger, and spices.
3. In a separate small bowl, combine hot water and rum.
4. In another small bowl, combine baking soda and molasses.
5. In a fourth bowl, cream shortening and sugar thoroughly.
6. Combine sifted ingredients, the water-rum mix, and the molasses mix with the creamed mixture.

*(continued on next page)*

7. Chill the dough for several hours.
8. Roll out 1/4-inch thick on floured board and cut with a 4-inch diameter cutter.
9. Bake for 10 to 12 minutes.

**Yield: 2 to 3 dozen cookies.**

NOTE: *Vary the rum to water ratio as the mood or season dictates.*

This recipe is great for creating holiday gingerbread cutouts. The dough holds a cookie cutter shape very well. I usually make Christmas bears. The yield will vary depending on the size of the cookie. The rum (I use spiced rum) seems to be the ingredient that woos my friends to these cookies. Even those who don't like gingerbread cookies tell me, "Oooh, I really like these."

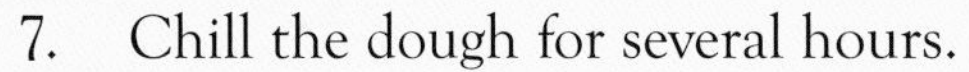

William Taft is the only man in U.S. history to serve as both President and Chief Justice of the Supreme Court (though not at the same time).

Taft was the first President to acquire automobiles for the White House. They were parked in the stable with the White House horses.

Taft was also the first President to pitch a ball to open the baseball season. The memorable pitch opened an American League game between Washington and Philadelphia.

# Woodrow Wilson (1856-1924)

## 28th President of the United States

(1913-1921)

ELLEN WILSON

WOODROW WILSON

EDITH WILSON

President Woodrow Wilson set the record for fastest rise to political office of all the Presidents. Within two years and 170 days, he went from a citizen who had never held public office to Governor of New Jersey and then to President of the United States. The entertaining tastes of the President and First Lady Ellen Wilson were simple. They chose to begin the presidential administration without an inaugural ball. But serving tea in the White House gardens delighted them—the fragrant roses, simmering teas, and soft chatter under blue skies, a simple but lasting pleasure.

In the evening, the Wilsons often served these meringue cookies, called Cream Cakes. When topped with fresh strawberries or raspberries, these Cream Cakes were elegant enough to serve as a formal White House dessert.

**President Wilson was the first President to**

**– cross the Atlantic while in office.**
**– conduct a presidential press conference.**
**– hold a doctorate degree (political science).**

**He was the second President to receive the Nobel Peace Prize.**

# Cream Cakes

3 EGG WHITES
1/8 TSP. SALT
1 CUP POWDERED SUGAR
1/4 TSP. LEMON EXTRACT

1. Preheat oven to 250°.
2. Beat whites stiffly with salt.
3. Add powdered sugar one tablespoon at a time while continuing to beat until mixture is as thick as a very thick batter.
4. Add lemon extract.
5. Drop by tablespoon onto cookie sheet covered with parchment paper.
6. Bake about 35 to 45 minutes until surface has hardened, but be careful that the cakes don't turn brown.
7. Turn the oven off.
8. Remove the cakes with a spatula.
9. Place them in pairs, bottom-to-bottom on a cookie sheet.
10. Return the sheet to the oven (which has been turned off) to dry briefly.

YIELD: 30 PAIRS OF CREAM CAKES.

### UNCLE SAM

Accounts vary about the origin of "Uncle Sam." The most likely account claims that the owner of a meat packing company named Samuel Wilson, and nicknamed Uncle Sam, put his initials on meat barrels that he supplied to American troops during the War of 1812. Since the initials U.S. also stand for the United States and represent property of the government, "Uncle Sam" became synonymous with the United States government.

In 1832, political cartoonists portrayed Uncle Sam as a tall, thin man. His most famous appearance comes from a World War I recruiting poster by James Montgomery Flagg. Congress adopted Uncle Sam as a national symbol in 1961.

President and Mrs. Wilson in the White House garden.

# Edith Bolling Wilson's Tea Cakes

*Soon after the death of First Lady Ellen Wilson, the President, while still serving in the White House, met and married Edith Bolling Galt. Interestingly, the new First Lady was a ninth generation descendant of Pocahontas. She frequently served these Tea Cakes at White House garden parties. Soon, however, as a result of the hardships of World War I, entertaining was curtailed. The Wilsons, along with the country, observed meatless and heatless days and gasless Sundays during the war.*

1/4 CUP BUTTER (1/2 STICK)
2 CUPS BROWN SUGAR
5 EGGS
1 TSP. BAKING SODA
1 TSP. SALT
1 TSP. NUTMEG
8 CUPS UNSIFTED FLOUR
SUGAR FOR DUSTING, IF DESIRED

1. Preheat oven to 375°.
2. In a large bowl, cream butter with sugar.
3. Beat in eggs, soda, nutmeg, and salt.
4. Stir in flour until dough is smooth.
5. Chill about 4 hours.
6. Place dough on a floured surface and roll out thin; cut with 3-inch cookie cutters.
7. Sprinkle cookies with sugar.
8. Bake on greased cookie sheets for about 6 to 10 minutes.

YIELD: 6 DOZEN TEA CAKES.

Served with fruit or a flavorful ice cream, these cookies are perfect for a tea or an easy dessert.

## 29th President of the United States

(1921-1923)

WARREN HARDING

FLORENCE HARDING

President Warren and First Lady Florence Harding started their administration by re-opening the White House. Closed during World War I, the White House filled with sunlight when the Hardings threw open the great doors to the mansion and to the lovely grounds. They held many dinners, receptions, and luncheons, eager to mingle with friends and share anecdotes from the war. At huge garden parties, they wore their Sunday best and served lemonade, punch, cookies, cakes, and sandwiches on long tables beneath striped awnings. Almond cookies were especially popular during the Harding presidency.

**Harding was the first President to**

**— ride in an automobile to his inauguration.**
**— put a radio set in the White House.**
**— travel to Alaska and Canada during his term of office.**

# Almond Cookies

*These cookies combine the nuttiness of almonds with the delicate zest of lemon. Chill the dough for these cookies about an hour before baking.*

1 3/4 cups sifted flour
2 eggs (used separately)
1 cup sugar
1 cup soft butter (2 sticks)
1/2 tsp. baking soda
Grated rind of 1 lemon
Pinch of salt
1/2 cup grated blanched almonds
Blanched almonds for garnish

1 Preheat oven to 350°.
2. In a bowl, sift flour and set aside.
3. In another bowl, mix thoroughly 1 whole egg, sugar, butter, soda, lemon rind, salt, and grated almonds.
4. Gradually work in the sifted flour.
5. Form the dough into 2 rolls about 2 inches in diameter.
6. Wrap in plastic wrap and chill for at least 1 hour.
7. Unwrap and cut into 1/8-inch slices.
8. Place sliced cookies on an ungreased baking sheet.
9. Brush with the other egg that has been beaten.
10. Decorate each cookie with 3 blanched almonds.
11. Bake for about 10 to12 minutes or until light brown.

Yield: 2 to 3 dozen cookies.

# Calvin Coolidge (1872-1933)

## *30th President of the United States*

(1923-1929)

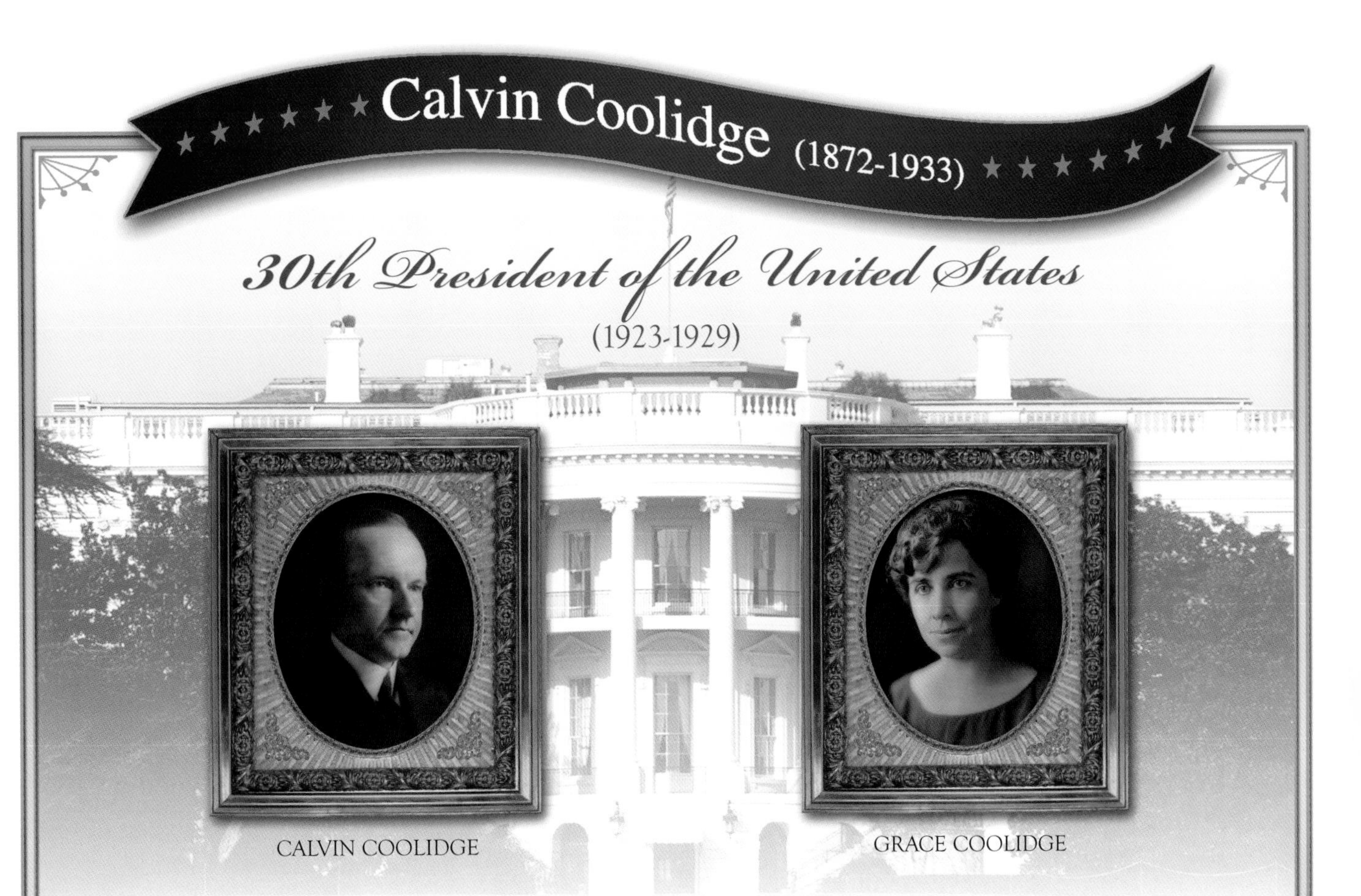

CALVIN COOLIDGE

GRACE COOLIDGE

The Coolidge Homestead in Plymouth Notch, Vermont, was the boyhood home of Calvin Coolidge as well as the place where he was sworn in as the thirtieth President of the United States. The swearing-in ceremony is related by William Jenney, Administrator of the President Calvin Coolidge State Historic Site.

> Vice President Coolidge was vacationing here when he received word of the unexpected death of President Warren Harding. Calvin's father, a notary public, administered the presidential oath of office at 2:47 a.m. on August 3, 1923. Years later, an inquisitive visitor asked the elder Coolidge, "How did you know you could administer the presidential oath to your own son?" The laconic Vermonter replied, "I didn't know that I couldn't." It is the only time in American history that a father has sworn in his son as President.

The village of Plymouth Notch remains virtually unchanged since the early 20th century with the rooms of the Homestead exactly as they were in 1923. Aurora Pierce, the housekeeper at the Coolidge Homestead, was the creator of presidential cookies known as Aurora Pierce's Famous Filled Cookies. According to the Vermont

Division for Historic Preservation, Aurora Pierce began her service at Plymouth Notch working for Colonel John Coolidge (the President's father). Following Colonel Coolidge's death in 1926, she stayed on for another 30 years. Aurora, a tiny lady of steel will, never accepted the easy life of electricity and "new fangled" plumbing, and so the house remained much as it was in 1923.

**President Coolidge made the first national radio broadcast from the White House.**

**During the holiday season of 1923, Calvin Coolidge lit the first National Christmas Tree on the Ellipse, the grassy area south of the White House.**

**President Coolidge is the only President to be born on Independence Day —July 4, 1872.**

The following recipes, including Aurora Pierce's Famous Filled Cookies, are from the *Coolidge-Country Cookbook: Early Recipes of the Coolidge Family, Their Plymouth Notch, Vermont Neighbors and Friends,* compiled by the Friends of the Calvin Coolidge Memorial Foundation, Plymouth, Vermont. The Calvin Coolidge Historic Site restaurant still bakes Grace Coolidge's Ice Box Cookies and serves them at special events to the delight of local townspeople and visitors.

# Grace Coolidge's Ice Box Cookies

1 cup butter or shortening (2 sticks)
(if shortening, use a little less and salt it)
2 cups brown sugar
3 1/2 cups flour
1 tsp. soda
1/2 tsp. salt
1 cup nut meats
2 eggs, well beaten

1. Preheat oven to 375°.
2. Cream butter and sugar.
3. Sift flour, soda, and salt 3 times.
4. Add nuts, add eggs and flour.
5. Mix all thoroughly and pack into mold (long narrow bread pan) and let stand overnight. Do not grease mold or baking pan.
6. Next day, unmold, slice very thin.
7. Bake for 10 minutes, and they will be nice and moist and chewy. Bake them a little longer if you want them crispy.

Yield: 4 dozen cookies.

# Aurora Pierce's Famous Filled Cookies

1 1/2 cups seedless raisins, chopped
1/2 cup sugar
1 Tbsp. flour
1/2 cup water
1/2 cup butter (1 stick)
1/2 tsp. vanilla extract
1 cup sugar
1 egg
3 1/2 cups sifted flour
2 tsp. cream of tartar
1 tsp. baking soda
1/2 cup milk
1 egg white for glaze

1. Preheat oven to 400°.
2. To make filling, combine chopped raisins, a mixture of 1/2 cup sugar and 1 Tbsp. flour, and 1/2 cup water.
3. Cook and stir until it thickens.
4. Cream together butter, vanilla extract, and sugar.
5. Beat in the egg.
6. Sift dry ingredients and add alternately with milk to the creamed mixture.
7. Blend well after each addition.
8. Roll dough 1/8-inch thick on a floured pastry canvas.
9. Cut with a 2-inch round cookie cutter.
10. Place on greased cookie sheet, add 1 teaspoon raisin filling and cover with another round of cookie dough. Press together with tines of a fork.
11. Brush tops with beaten egg white.
12. Bake for about 15 minutes.

Yield: 3 dozen cookies.

# Statue of Liberty

The Statue of Liberty, formally named *Liberty Enlightening the World,* is the foremost image symbolizing American freedom. France commissioned it to be a gift to the United States, representing the strong alliance between the two nations dating back to the Revolutionary War and the friendship between President George Washington and Frenchman Marquis de Lafayette. The Statue depicts a woman escaping the chains of tyranny. She holds a burning torch that represents liberty in her right hand. In her left hand is a tablet inscribed in Roman numerals, *July 4, 1776,* the day the United States declared its independence. Her flowing robes and the seven spikes of her crown signify the seven seas and continents.

The Statue was completed in Paris in 1884 and then dismantled into 350 pieces and packed in more than 200 wooden crates for its voyage to the United States. It took about four months to reassemble the Statue at its present location, Liberty Island, where President Grover Cleveland held the dedication ceremony on October 28, 1886. Over the years, the 305-foot high monument has undergone numerous renovations. President Calvin Coolidge designated the Statue of Liberty a National Monument on October 15, 1924.

# Herbert C. Hoover (1874-1964)

## *31st President of the United States*

(1929-1933)

HERBERT HOOVER

LOU HOOVER

*In 1931, President Hoover officially proclaimed the song, "The Star-Spangled Banner," America's official national anthem.*

*First Lady Lou Hoover served as National President of the Girl Scouts of the USA.*

President Herbert and First Lady Lou Hoover, believing that good things come in big packages, set the record for expansive and expensive entertaining in Washington. Energetic and ever hospitable, First Lady Lou would often conduct two teas during the same afternoon, one after the other, or even at the same time in different rooms, moving from one tea to the other to greet her guests. Three secretaries arranged the guest lists for First Lady Lou, often sending out three or four thousand handwritten invitations for a single reception. And the Hoovers' penchant for culinary extravagance didn't end at teas. Even when dining alone, the President and First Lady ate seven-course meals.

At her four o'clock teas, First Lady Lou served Lace Wafers, whether company came or not. These are simple cookies. Not very sweet, they make a light, cone-shaped teacake, perfect for a quiet afternoon moment.

# Mrs. Hoover's Lace Wafers

1/2 CUP MOLASSES, LIGHT OR DARK
1/2 CUP BUTTER (1 STICK)
3/4 CUP SUGAR
1 CUP FLOUR
1/2 TSP. GINGER

1. Preheat oven to 325°.
2. In a large saucepan, heat molasses to the boiling point.
3. Add butter, stirring constantly until butter melts.
4. In a bowl, sift dry ingredients.
5. Add sifted dry ingredients to the saucepan and continue stirring until all are blended.
6. Remove from heat.
7. Drop from a wooden spoon in small amounts about 2 inches apart on a cookie sheet.
8. Bake about 10 minutes.
9. While wafers are slightly warm, roll them around the handle of a wooden spoon to form a cone shape, allowing a minute to set.
10. Cool hardened wafers on a rack.

YIELD: 5 DOZEN WAFERS.

# Franklin D. Roosevelt (1882-1945)

## *32nd President of the United States*

(1933-1945)

FRANKLIN D. ROOSEVELT

ANNA ELEANOR ROOSEVELT

During his four administrations, President Franklin, with First Lady Eleanor Roosevelt always at his side, presided over large teas and receptions—frequent, fast, and furious events at the White House. As many as 5,000 guests would gather for tea on a single day. Constant last-minute changes kept White House staff hopping. A reception of 1,200 guests could skyrocket to a guest list of 4,200 almost overnight. White House staff often served tea for 300 guests at four o'clock in one room, just to quickly serve another tea upstairs at five-thirty. At one particular tea, the First Lady shook the hands of 1,175 people, while the 1,175 mouths ate 77 pounds of cookies and drank hundreds of gallons of punch—all within 30 minutes! Both First Lady Eleanor and her White House housekeeper, Mrs. Henrietta Nesbitt, agreed that this tea party was their speediest ever.

Mrs. Nesbitt, who went on to write a book about life with the Roosevelts, recalls intimate teas on the White House front porch, with the First Lady pouring. These small teas were sit-down affairs at quaint drop-leaf tables adorned with beautiful lace cloths and tiny nosegays of flowers. Served to these lucky guests were cinnamon toast, tiny sandwiches, cookies, little cakes, candy, and nuts—only that which could be eaten with one's fingers.

President Franklin Roosevelt is the only President to be elected to a fourth term. His inauguration on January 20, 1945, was celebrated by a lunch for 2,000 guests. Then at four-thirty, White House staff held a tea for 1,800 new guests and served 100 unfrosted marble cakes and 200 dozen cookies (that's 2,400 cookies).

In *The Presidential Cookbook, Feeding the Roosevelts and Their Guests,* Mrs. Nesbitt writes that while she was always on the lookout for new cookie recipes to serve at the First Family's large teas and receptions, she also baked thousands of cookies for veterans and hospital groups, delivered in style by the White House.

Because butter was in short supply during the war, the First Family turned to macaroon recipes of every possible kind, which used ingredients such as coconut, chocolate, cornflakes, dates, nuts, and bread crumbs instead of butter. When butter was available, however, Honey Drops were a favorite accompaniment to tea.

***President Roosevelt, known as FDR, was related to eleven former Presidents:***

***George Washington***
***John Adams***
***James Madison***
***John Quincy Adams***
***Martin Van Buren***
***William Harrison***
***Zachary Taylor***
***Ulysses Grant***
***Benjamin Harrison***
***Theodore Roosevelt***
***William Taft***

# Honey Drops

1 cup sugar
1 cup honey
1 cup butter (2 sticks)
2 tsp. baking powder
1 tsp. salt
1 egg
1/2 tsp. cinnamon
1/2 tsp. almond flavoring
1/2 cup chopped walnuts
1/4 cup chopped orange peel
About 3 cups flour

1. Preheat oven to 325°.
2. Mix all ingredients except the flour.
3. Add enough flour so that the mixture can be rolled into balls and placed on a cookie sheet without running.
4. After placing rolled balls on cookie sheet, bake for 12 to 14 minutes.

Yield: 12 dozen drops.

The honey flavor transforms these simple cookies into tasty little drops. Try different types of honey to create a variety of taste treats. Each time I baked this recipe, I needed to add more flour than suggested in the recipe. Add enough flour so that fairly firm balls the size of walnuts can be formed. Test bake one or two cookies to check for consistency.

*The Fourth of July has been celebrated annually since 1776. But not until 1941, 165 years later, did it become a legal holiday under President Roosevelt's signature.*

*President Roosevelt was the first President to appear on television.*

# Almond Crescents

*These crescent-shaped cookies, rich with butter, almond flavor, and a sweet sprinkle of powdered sugar, melt in your mouth.*

2/3 CUP FLOUR
1 CUP GROUND ALMONDS
1/4 CUP POWDERED SUGAR
1/2 CUP BUTTER (1 STICK)
1/2 TSP. ALMOND EXTRACT
POWDERED SUGAR FOR SPRINKLING AFTER BAKING

1. Preheat oven to 325°.
2. Mix flour, almonds, and sugar.
3. In a small bowl, cream butter and almond extract.
4. Add butter to flour mixture.
5. Knead cookie dough with hands until smooth.
6. Roll into a 2-inch-thick roll. Slice.
7. Form slices into crescents about 4 inches long, tapering at each end.
8. Place crescents on an ungreased cookie sheet.
9. Bake about 15 minutes until crescents are white.
10. Cool on a rack.
11. Sprinkle cookies with powdered sugar.

YIELD: 3 DOZEN CRESCENTS.

*Eleanor Roosevelt served longer than any other First Lady. The "First Lady of the World" is remembered for her wisdom, among her sayings,*

*"The future belongs to those who believe in the beauty of their dreams."*

*"You must do the things you think you cannot do."*

# Harry S. Truman (1884-1972)

## 33rd President of the United States

(1945-1953)

HARRY S. TRUMAN

ELIZABETH "BESS" TRUMAN

*President Truman hosted the first television tour of the White House.*

*He also gave the first presidential address telecast from the White House in 1947.*

The author of a 1940's newspaper article nicknamed President Harry and First Lady Bess Truman "The Cookie Lady and Her Husband." The young reporter for the *Kansas City Times,* Tom Leathers, recounted his unusual encounters with the presidential couple, which occurred on two consecutive Christmas days.

Both times, the Trumans had returned to their home in Independence, Missouri, for the holidays. The reporter, assigned to loiter in front of the Truman house just in case a newsworthy event should occur, lingered and waited. (These were the days when the press did not besiege the First Family!) Hoping for a story, he stood during the chilly Christmas days outside the house, waiting and watching.

Finally one morning, First Lady Bess Truman waved vigorously from the window for the reporter to come into the house. He followed her into the kitchen where she offered him a paper plate with cookies and a cup of hot chocolate. "Would you like to say hello to Mr. Truman?" she asked him, leading him to the living room. The President was sitting in a rocking chair, reading a history book.

He wished the reporter a merry Christmas. The First Lady then escorted the stunned reporter outside with his cookies.

The next Christmas he enjoyed the same encounter, but the drink was hot cider and the conversation a bit longer. Tom Leathers never forgot the President and First Lady, their delicious cookies and hot drinks, and the hospitality extended to him on those wintry Christmas days.

The Harry Truman National Historic Site provided the following recipes. Handwritten by First Lady Bess Truman, the three recipe cards show flour smudges, buttery fingerprints, and rumpled corners—telltale signs of favorite Truman recipes.

Coconut Cookies

Cream 1/2 cup butter & 1 c. sugar.
Add 1 egg 1/4 c. milk 1/2 c. Dom. coconut 2 cups flour. 1 teas bkg pd. Roll thin & bake in quick oven.

Kisses (Ella Ross)

7 eggs beaten very lightly
1 pt sugar –
Save 2 tablesp of sugar to put in at last
Beat rest of sugar & eggs together good
add pinch of salt
Bake on brown unbuttered paper in slow oven about 45 minutes

Butter Scotch Cookies

2 c. brown sugar
1 scant cup butter & lard mixed
2 eggs.
1 teas. cream tartar
1 " soda
1 " vanilla
4 cups flour
1 " nuts
Mix all [illegible] to let

These are the handwritten cookie recipes of First Lady Bess Truman, provided by the Harry S. Truman National Historic Site, Independence, Missouri.

# Coconut Cookies

1/2 CUP BUTTER (1 STICK)
1 CUP SUGAR
1 EGG
1/4 CUP MILK
1/2 CUP DRIED COCONUT
2 CUPS FLOUR
1 TSP. BAKING POWDER

1. Preheat oven to 375°.
2. Cream butter and sugar.
3. Add egg, milk, coconut, flour, and baking powder.
4. Roll to 1/4-inch thickness and cut into shapes with a cookie cutter.
5. Place cookies on a greased cookie sheet and bake 10 to12 minutes.
6. Cool on a rack.

YIELD: 3 DOZEN COOKIES.

After baking, add flair and extra sweetness to these simple cookies by brushing them with honey and sprinkling the tops with coconut. Broil just long enough to toast the coconut to light brown.

# Kisses

4 EGG WHITES
1-POUND BOX OF POWDERED SUGAR (3 1/2 CUPS)
1 TSP. LEMON JUICE
PARCHMENT PAPER

1. Preheat oven to 250°.
2. Beat egg whites until very stiff.
3. Beat in sugar and lemon juice.
4. Drop by teaspoon on cookie sheets lined with parchment paper.
5. Bake for about 30 minutes until kisses are set but not brown.

YIELD: 3 DOZEN KISSES.

I adapted this original recipe by adding lemon juice for a lemony taste. For variation, add 2 cups chopped walnuts or chocolate chips. At holidays, top each kiss with colored sugar or a red cinnamon heart.

# Butterscotch Cookies

*Allow the dough for these Butterscotch Cookies to chill overnight in the refrigerator before slicing and baking the next day.*

2 CUPS LIGHT BROWN SUGAR, PACKED
1 CUP SOFTENED BUTTER (2 STICKS)
2 EGGS
1 TSP. CREAM OF TARTAR
1 TSP. SODA
1 TSP VANILLA
4 CUPS FLOUR
1 CUP CHOPPED NUTS, ANY VARIETY

1. Preheat oven to 350°.
2. Mix all ingredients.
3. Form dough into two 2-inch rolls and cover them with plastic wrap. Let chill overnight in the refrigerator.
4. Slice into rounds about 1/4-inch thick.
5. Bake 10 to 12 minutes.
6. Remove cookies to a rack to cool thoroughly.

YIELD: 3 TO 4 DOZEN COOKIES.

# Dwight D. Eisenhower (1890-1969)

## *34th President of the United States*

(1953-1961)

DWIGHT D. EISENHOWER

MAMIE EISENHOWER

> ***President and First Lady Eisenhower began the tradition of sending the White House Christmas card to the public.***

Although they preferred to entertain small, intimate parties as part of their presidential duties, President Dwight and First Lady Mamie Eisenhower hosted more royalty and heads of state than many previous First Families. However, for those evenings when official dining was not planned, the President and First Lady relished their meals alone. Like most other Americans at the time, they enjoyed their dinners served on trays so they could watch television as they ate.

President Eisenhower, with his culinary skills and interest in cookbooks, knew much about the history of the White House kitchen and considered himself an amateur chef. The First Lady, on the other hand, laughingly called herself "a cooking-school dropout," claiming she could make only mayonnaise and fudge. Growing up with the convenience of a family cook, she probably ventured into the kitchen only to look for a cookie. Despite her lack of culinary talent, the First Lady kept a recipe file of numerous Eisenhower family specialties. The following is a holiday recipe that was a favorite of the First Family.

# Sugar Cookies from Mamie's White House Recipe Files

1/2 cup butter (1 stick)
1 cup sugar
2 egg yolks, well beaten
1 Tbsp. cream
1 tsp. vanilla
1/2 tsp. salt
1 tsp. baking powder
1 1/2 cups flour
Sugar for dusting

1. Preheat oven to 350°.
2. In a small bowl, mix flour, baking powder, and salt.
3. In a large bowl, cream butter, adding sugar slowly. Mix until fluffy.
4. Stir in well-beaten egg yolks and vanilla.
5. Add sifted dry ingredients alternately with the cream.
6. Chill cookie dough for one hour. Roll out on a floured surface and cut in any desired shape.
7. Sprinkle with sugar before baking.
8. Place cookies on an ungreased cookie sheet.
9. Bake 10 to12 minutes.

Yield: 3 dozen cookies.

*These cookies can be cut into star shapes and decorated with red, white, and blue sprinkles.*

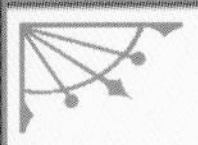

# The Flag of the United States

On June 14, 1777, the Continental Congress passed the first of several Flag Acts, establishing that the flag of the United States have thirteen stripes in red and white and thirteen stars to represent the colonies. Each color symbolizes America's values: red for hardiness and valor, white for purity and innocence, and blue for vigilance, perseverance and justice. The American flag is frequently called the Star-Spangled Banner or the Stars and Stripes because of its stars, stripes, and red, white, and blue colors.

Most historians believe that Congressman Francis Hopkinson designed the first flag rather than Betsy Ross. In 1795, Congress provided for 15 stripes and 15 stars. Then in 1818, President James Monroe signed another act providing for 13 stripes as well as one star for each state to be added on the Fourth of July following the admission of each new state. In 1912, President William Taft set the proportions of the flag. In 1949, President Truman signed an Act of Congress designating June 14 as National Flag Day.

# The Pledge of Allegiance

In 1892, President Benjamin Harrison officially proclaimed that the pledge of allegiance be recited on Columbus Day. Historical legend has it that the Boston magazine, *The Youth's Companion,* printed thousands of leaflets with the first Pledge of Allegiance written on them. The magazine sent them out to public schools across the country for students to read on Columbus Day that year. The first Pledge of Allegiance read:

***I pledge allegiance to my Flag and to the Republic for which it stands—one nation indivisible—with liberty and justice for all.***

The first National Flag Conference substituted for "my Flag" the words "the Flag of the United States." In 1924, "of America" was added. In 1954, President Dwight Eisenhower inserted the words "under God."

The following is our present Pledge of Allegiance:

***I pledge allegiance to the Flag of the United States of America and to the Republic for which it stands, one nation under God, indivisible, with liberty and justice for all.***

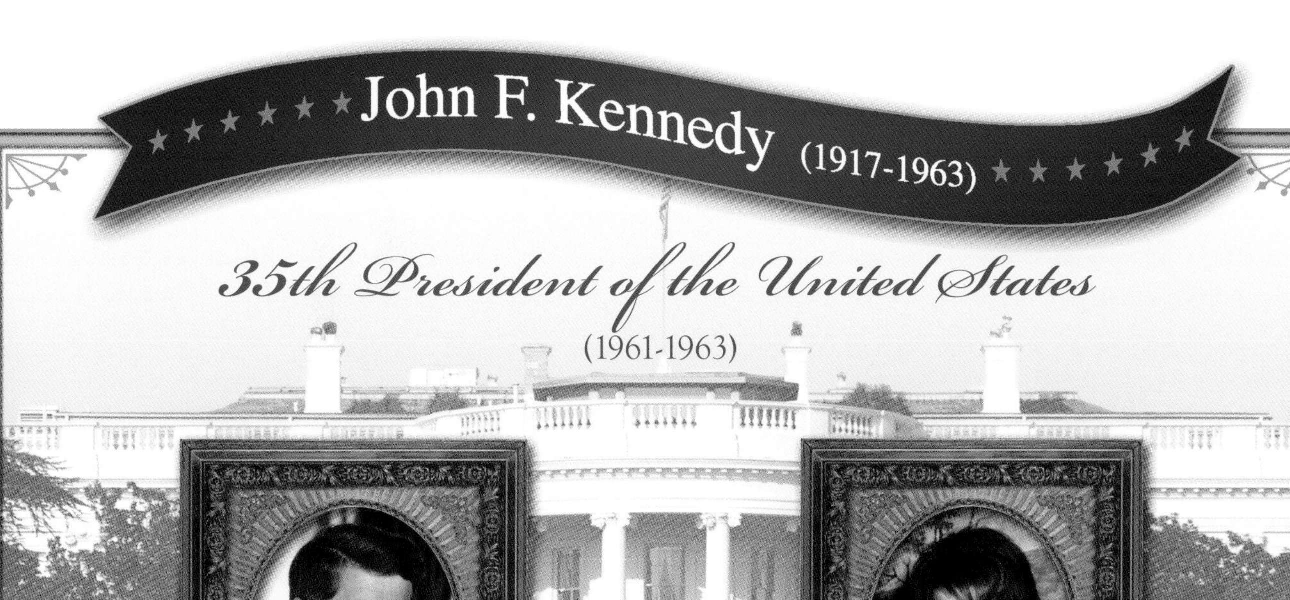

# John F. Kennedy (1917-1963)

## 35th President of the United States

(1961-1963)

JOHN F. KENNEDY

JACQUELINE KENNEDY

Cookies were festive additions at White House events during the presidency of President John and First Lady Jacqueline Kennedy. Devoted parents, the Kennedys delighted their children by putting an 18-foot Christmas tree in the White House and decorating the branches with gingerbread men, candy canes, dolls, and toys. The cuisine for the First Family had a notable French flair, their meals and desserts prepared daily by their French chef. When the Kennedys arrived at the White House, their French chef renamed these popular delicate cookies, Tuiles. Tuiles is the French word for "tiles," which these cookies resemble.

*President Kennedy set a goal for the United States to put a man on the moon. This historical event occurred on July 20, 1969.*

*First Lady Jacqueline Kennedy approved the creation of the White House Historical Association, which preserves the heritage of the White House.*

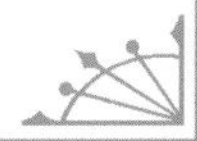

# Chocolate Almond Tuiles

1/2 cup butter (1 stick)
1 cup powdered sugar
4 egg whites
1/2 tsp. almond extract
1/2 cup cake flour
1/2 cup cocoa

1. Preheat oven to 325°.
2. Make a circle template by cutting a circle in a thin piece of cardboard or plastic (about 3 1/2-inch diameter).
3. In a bowl, cream butter and sugar together with an electric mixer on medium speed.
4. Beat in the egg whites, one at a time.
5. Beat in almond extract.
6. Blend flour with cocoa.
7. Add flour and cocoa mixture to butter mixture at low speed until just blended. Do not overmix.
8. Chill batter for at least one hour.
9. Line a cookie sheet with parchment paper. Place the tem plate on it.
10. Using a small spatula, spread a small amount of batter evenly over the template. Carefully lift the template off.
11. Bake only 4 to 6 Tuiles at a time for 8 to 10 minutes until edges are light brown.
12. While the cookies are still warm, bend each one over a rolling pin or glass so that they resemble curved tiles.
13. Let each cookie cool on the rolling pin for 1 to 2 minutes to harden.
14. Remove and cool on a wire rack.

Yield: 2 dozen Tuiles.

# Lyndon B. Johnson (1908-1973)

## 36th President of the United States

(1963-1969)

LYNDON B. JOHNSON

CLAUDIA "LADY BIRD" JOHNSON

President Lyndon and First Lady Lady Bird Johnson brought warm, down-home Texan hospitality and flavor to White House food and entertaining. They staged the first cookout at the mansion and served the first state dinner in the Rose Garden. All the members of the First Family shared the initials "LBJ": Lyndon Baines Johnson, Lady Bird Johnson, Lynda Bird Johnson, Luci Baines Johnson, and even the dogs, Little Beagles Johnson, called Him and Her. The Johnson family often relaxed at the LBJ ranch in Texas and enjoyed Lemon Squares and Chocolate Nut Drop Cookies. Following are the First Lady's recipes noted on her personal stationery.

*President Johnson signed the Civil Rights Act on July 2, 1964, in a televised ceremony at the White House. The law protects the right to vote, assures access to public places, and withholds federal funds from discriminatory programs.*

LEMON SQUARES

2 CUPS FLOUR

1/4 CUP SUGAR

1 CUP BUTTER

MIX FIRST 3 INGREDIENTS AS FOR PIE CRUST. PAT INTO AN 9 X 18 JELLY ROLL PAN. BAKE AT 350 UNTIL VERY LIGHT BROWN -- ABOUT 15 MINUTES.

2 CUPS SUGAR

1 TSP. BAKING POWDER

4 TBSP. FLOUR

3 BEATEN EGGS

JUICE AND RIND OF 2 LEMONS

MIX INGREDIENTS IN ORDER GIVEN AND POUR OVER BAKED CRUST. BAKE AT 350 FOR 15 - 20 MINUTES OR UNTIL SET. SPRINKLE WITH POWDERED SUGAR.

*MOLLIE PARNIS LIVINGSTON, A DEAR FRIEND OF MRS. JOHNSON'S, GAVE HER THIS RECIPE FOR LEMON SQUARES AND IT IS ONE OF HER FAVORITES. THE COOK AT THE LBJ RANCH KEEPS THEM IN THE FREEZER SO MRS. JOHNSON WILL ALWAYS HAVE THEM WHEN SHE WANTS A SNACK OR A DELICIOUS ENDING TO A MEAL!*

**MRS. LYNDON B. JOHNSON'S RECIPE FOR...**

**CHOCOLATE NUT DROP COOKIES**

**1 CUP BUTTER** — **2 CUPS LIGHT BROWN SUGAR**

**1/2 CUP EGGS (2 OR 3)** — **1 CUP MILK**

**3 CUPS CAKE FLOUR** — **1 TEASPOON SODA**

**1 TEASPOON SALT** — **4 SQUARES CHOCOLATE**

2 CUPS WALNUTS, CHOPPED — 2 TEASPOONS VANILLA

CREAM BUTTER, THEN ADD THE SIFTED BROWN SUGAR GRADUALLY. CREAM UNTIL LIGHT AND FLUFFY.

ADD THE WELL-BEATEN EGGS TO THE CREAMED INGREDIENTS.

SIFT TOGETHER THE DRY INGREDIENTS AND ADD WITH MILK ALTERNATELY. MIX UNTIL SMOOTH.

ADD MELTED CHOCOLATE, CHOPPED NUTS AND VANILLA. FOLD INTO MIXTURE.

DROP BY TEASPOONSFULS (ONE INCH APART) ON OILED BAKING SHEET.

BAKE AT 375 DEGREES FOR 12 TO 15 MINUTES.

MAKES 6 DOZEN.

# Lemon Squares

*This recipe for Lemon Squares was a particular favorite of the First Family. The cook at the LBJ ranch kept these tangy bars in the freezer so that whenever a presidential sweet tooth struck, they would be available.*

## Crust

2 cups flour
1/4 cup sugar
1 cup butter (2 sticks)

1. Preheat oven to 350°.
2. Mix first 3 ingredients as for pie crust.
3. Pat into a 9 x 18 x 1-inch greased cookie sheet.
4. Bake for about 15 minutes until very light brown.

## Filling

2 cups sugar
1 tsp. baking powder
4 Tbsp. flour
3 beaten eggs
Juice and grated rind of 2 lemons
Powdered sugar to sprinkle on top

1. Mix ingredients in the order given and pour over baked crust.
2. Bake for 15 to 20 minutes or until set.
3. When the pan is cool, cut into squares and sprinkle them with powdered sugar.

Yield: 24 squares.

# Chocolate Nut Drop Cookies

1 CUP BUTTER (2 STICKS)
2 CUPS LIGHT BROWN SUGAR, PACKED
1/2 CUP EGGS (2 OR 3), WELL BEATEN
3 CUPS CAKE FLOUR
1 TSP. SODA
1 TSP. SALT
1 CUP MILK
FOUR 1-OUNCE SQUARES UNSWEETENED CHOCOLATE, MELTED
2 CUPS WALNUTS, CHOPPED
2 TSP. VANILLA

1. Preheat oven to 375°.
2. In small bowl, cream butter, adding brown sugar gradually.
3. Cream until light and fluffy.
4. Add the well-beaten eggs to the creamed ingredients.
5. In another bowl, sift together the dry ingredients.
6. Add creamed mixture to dry ingredients alternately with milk. Mix until smooth.
7. Add melted chocolate to combined mixture along with chopped nuts and vanilla.
8. Drop by teaspoon 1-inch apart on a greased cookie sheet.
9. Bake for 12 to 15 minutes.

YIELD: 6 DOZEN COOKIES.

*While living at the White House, President and Mrs. Johnson erected two 20-foot Christmas trees during the holidays. One of them was a cookie tree hung with decorative and edible cookies.*

# Richard M. Nixon (1913-1994)

## *37th President of the United States*

(1969-1974)

RICHARD M. NIXON

PATRICIA NIXON

At a ladies' party to honor Republican Party workers, President Richard and First Lady Pat Nixon decided to keep the menu simple, serving only cookies and lemonade–simply abundant, that is, with 25,000 cookies and 225 gallons of lemonade. Pity the poor cook trying to keep count of all those cookies.

*On July 20, 1969, President Nixon spoke from the Oval Office to astronauts Neil Armstrong and "Buzz" Aldrin as they walked on the moon. Armstrong and Aldrin were the first men to walk on the moon.*

# Sequoia Brownies

*Named after the presidential yacht, the* USS Sequoia, *these brownies were often served to the President and First Lady and their guests as they cruised the Potomac. Prince Charles and Princess Anne enjoyed them aboard the* USS Sequoia *during their visit to Washington, D.C., in July 1970, as did other dignitaries during their brownie cruises.*

2 squares (2 ounces) unsweetened chocolate
1/2 cup butter (1 stick)
1 cup sugar
2 eggs
1 tsp. vanilla
1/2 cup sifted flour
1 cup chopped walnuts
Chocolate frosting or powdered sugar, as desired

1. Preheat oven to 350°.
2. Grease an 8-inch square pan and dust lightly with flour.
3. Melt chocolate in the top of a double boiler set over hot water or in a microwave oven. Let cool.
4. Cream butter with sugar.
5. Add eggs and beat well.
6. Blend in melted chocolate, vanilla, and flour.
7. Stir in nuts.
8. Pour into prepared pan.
9. Bake for 35 minutes.
10. Let cool completely on wire rack before frosting or dusting with powdered sugar.
11. Cut into 16 even squares.

Yield: 16 brownies.

You do not have to be cruising in presidential style to enjoy these brownies. Serve them with vanilla ice cream or whipped cream as a decadent treat. Sometimes I cut the brownies into tiny bite-sized squares for a large party.

*The Presidential Yacht,* USS Sequoia, *served eight Presidents from Hoover to Ford.*

# Pat Nixon's Christmas Tree Cookies

4 CUPS SIFTED FLOUR
2/3 TSP. BAKING SODA
1/4 TSP. EACH CINNAMON, ALLSPICE, GINGER, AND MACE
2 TBSP. DARK CORN SYRUP
1/2 CUP SUGAR
1 EGG
1 CUP HONEY
COLORED SUGAR OR MELTED CHOCOLATE TO DECORATE

1. Preheat oven to 350°.
2. In a small bowl, combine flour, baking soda, and spices.
3. In a large bowl, blend honey, syrup, sugar, and egg.
4. Combine the dry ingredients with the honey mixture.
5. Roll dough to 1/4-inch thickness.
6. Cut into desired shapes with cookie cutters.
7. Brush the cookies with water and sprinkle with colored sugar, or after baking them, dip them in melted chocolate.
8. Bake 10 to 12 minutes or until firm.

YIELD: 5 DOZEN COOKIES.

These cookies make cute Christmas ornaments. While the cookies are still warm and soft from the oven, make little holes near the top of each cookie. Make sure the holes are large enough for the string or ribbon.

# Gerald R. Ford (1913- )

## 38th President of the United States

(1974-1977)

GERALD FORD

ELIZABETH "BETTY" FORD

President Gerald and First Lady Betty Ford brought a friendly, relaxed lifestyle to the White House. While the First Family preferred all-American food, the First Lady liked to incorporate the presidential recipes of earlier administrations into official dining events. Brunches were especially popular during the Ford presidency. According to First Lady Betty, the President's favorite food is ice cream, especially butter pecan. Possibly he enjoys these Double Chocolate Chip Cookies along with his ice cream.

*In 1975, President Ford authorized the redesign of the official Coat of Arms, the United States Seal, and the Flag of the Vice President of the United States. This design is still used today.*

# Double Chocolate Chip Cookies

1 CUP BUTTER, SOFTENED (2 STICKS)
1 3/4 CUPS SUGAR
2 EGGS
2 TSP. BRANDY OR VANILLA
1 OUNCE UNSWEETENED BAKING CHOCOLATE, MELTED
1/4 CUP SOUR CREAM
2 CUPS FLOUR
3/4 CUP COCOA
1/2 TSP. BAKING SODA
1/4 TSP. BAKING POWDER
1/2 TSP. SALT
2 CUPS WHITE CHOCOLATE CHIPS
1 CUP CHOPPED BRAZIL NUTS OR ALMONDS

1. Preheat the oven to 350°.
2. In a large mixing bowl, beat together the butter and sugar until light and fluffy.
3. Add eggs one at a time, beating well after each addition.
4. Beat in the brandy or vanilla.
5. Stir the melted chocolate and sour cream into the creamed mixture.
6. In a medium bowl, sift together the flour, cocoa, baking soda, baking powder, and salt.
7. Add dry ingredients to creamed mixture.
8. Stir in the white chocolate chips and nuts.
9. Drop the batter by tablespoon onto ungreased cookie sheets.
10. Bake 12 to 14 minutes.
11. Remove from oven and cool 5 minutes.
12. Transfer cookies to wire rack and cool completely.

YIELD: 5 DOZEN COOKIES.

*Gerald Ford served as Vice-President and President without being elected to either post. As Vice-President, he stepped in to complete President Richard Nixon's term.*

*Ford was the first President to have been an Eagle Scout.*

# James E. Carter (1924- )

## 39th President of the United States

(1977-1981)

JIMMY CARTER

ROSALYNN CARTER

As natives of Georgia, President Jimmy and First Lady Rosalynn Carter are particularly fond of cookies made from the delicious pecans and peanuts so popular in their home state.

Introduced as Pecan Diamonds by White House pastry chef, Henry Haller, these cookies became a special request of the First Family. The Carter administration served many batches of the rich pecan cookies at official teas and at Sunday afternoon receptions after concerts and performances. President and First Lady Carter offered them when they entertained guests for dinner, adding a delicious touch of festive southern hospitality to the evening.

*President Carter was awarded the Nobel Peace Prize in 2002. He is the third President to receive this honor.*

*President Carter, a speed reader, has been clocked at 2,000 words per minute.*

# Pecan Squares

*I adapted this recipe from* The White House Family Cookbook *by Henry Haller with Virginia Aronson. Originally the cookies were cut into diamonds, yielding about 200 diamonds, a sufficient number for White House guest lists but far more than needed for the typical home! I simply cut them into little squares. At the holidays I serve them instead of traditional pecan pie. The scrumptious filling makes it nearly impossible to eat just one.*

## Pastry Crust

1 CUP BUTTER (2 STICKS)
1/2 CUP SHORTENING
7/8 CUP SUGAR
2 EGGS
1 TSP. VANILLA
4 1/2 CUPS FLOUR
1/2 TSP. BAKING POWDER
PINCH OF SALT

1. Preheat oven to 350°.
2. In a large mixing bowl, cream butter and shortening with sugar.
3. Blend in eggs and vanilla.
4. Add flour, baking powder, and salt.
5. Mix just until combined (do not overmix).
6. Pat pastry into a 10 1/2 x 15 1/2 x 1-inch cookie sheet.
7. Prick pastry with a fork.
8. Bake for 15 minutes.
9. Cool crust while preparing the filling.

## Filling

1 cup butter (2 sticks)
1/2 cup light brown sugar, packed
1/4 cup granulated sugar
3/4 cup honey
4 cups chopped pecans
1/4 cup heavy cream

1. In a saucepan, combine butter, honey, and granulated and light brown sugars.
2. Bring to a boil over medium heat; let boil for 3 minutes. Do not stir during this time.
3. Remove saucepan from heat.
4. Fold in chopped nuts and heavy cream.
5. Spread hot pecan filling over baked pastry crust.
6. Bake at 350° for 20 to 30 minutes or until bottom crust is completely cooked. Filling will still be soft.
7. Let cool completely on a wire rack.
8. Use a sharp knife to cut into squares.

Yield: 45 squares.

# Amy Carter's Peanut Butter Cookies

*Because these peanut butter cookies were such a favorite of their daughter, Amy, President and First Lady Carter kept fresh batches in a boot-shaped cookie jar in the White House kitchen.*

1 CUP BUTTER (2 STICKS)
1/2 CUP CHUNKY OR SMOOTH PEANUT BUTTER
1 CUP GRANULATED SUGAR
1 CUP LIGHT BROWN SUGAR, PACKED
1/4 TSP. SALT
2 EGGS
1 TSP. BAKING SODA
1/4 CUP WARM WATER
3 CUPS SIFTED FLOUR

1. Preheat oven to 350°.
2. In a large mixing bowl, cream together butter and peanut butter.
3. Beat in the granulated and light brown sugars and salt.
4. Beat in eggs, one at a time.
5. In a small bowl, dissolve baking soda in warm water. Add to the butter-sugar mixture and stir well.
6. Stir in flour. Mix until dough is smooth.
7. Wrap dough in plastic wrap and refrigerate for 1 hour or until dough is firm enough to be workable.
8. Roll dough by hand into 1-inch balls.
9. Arrange balls on ungreased cookie sheets, leaving 1 to 2 inches between cookies.
10. Gently press each ball flat with the tines of a fork; press each cookie again, crosswise, to flatten to 1/4-inch thickness and to create the characteristic crisscross pattern.
11. To prevent fork from sticking, occasionally dip it in flour.
12. Bake for 15 minutes or until golden brown.
13. Let cookies stand for 10 minutes before transferring them to wire racks to cool completely.
14. Store in a tightly covered container.

YIELD: 5 DOZEN COOKIES.

Make large cookies by forming the dough into large balls about the size of golf balls. Bake about 20 to 25 minutes until light brown.

# Rosalynn Carter's Raisin-Oatmeal Cookies

*These raisin-oatmeal cookies are another favorite of the Carter family. Rosalynn Carter contributed her recipe to the* American Heart Association Cookbook, *4th Edition.*

1 CUP FLOUR, SIFTED
1/2 TSP. BAKING SODA
1/4 TSP. CINNAMON
1 1/2 CUPS QUICK-COOKING ROLLED OATS
2 EGG WHITES, SLIGHTLY BEATEN
1 CUP LIGHT BROWN SUGAR, PACKED
1/3 CUP VEGETABLE OIL
1/2 CUP SKIM MILK
1 TSP. VANILLA
1 CUP RAISINS

***First Lady Rosalynn works on behalf of women's rights and programs for the mentally ill.***

1. Preheat oven to 375°.
2. In a large bowl, sift together flour, baking soda, and cinnamon.
3. Stir in the oats.
4. In another bowl, combine egg whites, brown sugar, oil, milk, vanilla, and raisins.
5. Add the flour mixture to the egg mixture. Mix well.
6. Drop batter a teaspoon at a time onto a greased cookie sheet.
7. Bake for 12 to 15 minutes, depending on texture desired. A shorter baking time results in a chewy soft cookie, a longer time in a crisp one.

YIELD: 3 DOZEN COOKIES.

## *40th President of the United States*

(1981-1989)

RONALD REAGAN

NANCY REAGAN

Simplicity was characteristic of the entertainment style and taste of President Ronald and First Lady Nancy Reagan. And the simple but well-loved cookie was an integral part of two memorable meals for this First Family. The day after the presidential inauguration, President and First Lady Reagan invited some close friends to lunch upstairs in the White House. The meal included celery, broth, cheese soufflé, kirsch-sprinkled fruit salad, and cookies. This simple, delicious meal was reminiscent of another special lunch at Pacific Palisades the day after Ronald Reagan's election as Governor of California. That lunch of homemade lentil soup and a cheese sandwich on seven-grain health bread was capped off with cookies and fruit.

The former personal secretary for President Reagan, Kathy Osborne, recalls that he always had chocolate chip cookies on hand. The presidential staff even arranged to have his favorite kind, chocolate chip cookies, available upon

*In his youth, President Reagan worked as a lifeguard during the summer. He is credited with saving 77 swimmers.*

*The President and First Lady were screen actors when they met and married.*

*At age 69, President Ronald Reagan was the oldest man to be inaugurated. He was not only the oldest man when he was elected, but also the oldest when he left office at age 77.*

arrival when the President traveled. The President's favorite dessert, however, was fresh fruit or ice cream served with Nancy Reagan's Vienna Chocolate Bars or her Brownies. In fact, his love for ice cream prompted him in 1984 to declare July as National Ice Cream Month, citing the food's "nutritious and wholesome" qualities.

# Vienna Chocolate Bars

*Elegant yet easy to make, these bars are a delicious blend of chocolate and raspberry with the surprise of a crunchy meringue topping.*

1 CUP BUTTER (2 STICKS)
1 1/2 CUPS SUGAR
2 1/2 CUPS FLOUR
1/4 TSP. SALT
1 CUP SEMISWEET CHOCOLATE CHIPS
2 EGG YOLKS
ONE 10-OUNCE JAR RASPBERRY JELLY
4 EGG WHITES
2 CUPS FINELY CHOPPED NUTS

1. Preheat oven to 350°.
2. Cream the butter, only 1/2 cup of sugar, and 2 egg yolks.
3. Add the flour and salt and knead with fingers.
4. Pat batter flat onto a greased cookie sheet.
5. Bake for 15 to 20 minutes until lightly browned.
6. Remove the cookie sheet from the oven.
7. Spread jelly across the baked cookie crust, and top with chocolate chips.
8. Beat egg whites until they are stiff. Fold in remaining sugar and nuts.
9. Gently spread the egg white mixture on top of the jelly and chocolate chips.
10. Bake again for about 25 minutes.
11. Cut into squares or bars.

YIELD: 2 DOZEN BARS.

*The Secret Service gave First Lady Nancy Reagan the code name Rainbow.*

*First Lady Nancy Reagan wrote the book* To Love a Child, *about the Foster Grandparent Program, which she enthusiastically supports.*

# Nancy Reagan's Brownies

3 squares semisweet baking chocolate
2 squares unsweetened baking chocolate
1 1/2 cups butter (3 sticks)
6 eggs
2 cups granulated sugar
2/3 cup cake flour
1 1/2 tsp. salt
1 tsp. baking powder
1 Tbsp. vanilla
2 cups finely chopped pecans
Powdered sugar

1. Preheat oven to 350°.
2. Melt chocolate and butter in top of double boiler and then cool.
3. In a small bowl, beat eggs and sugar until a light color.
4. Add chocolate mixture to egg mixture.
5. In another bowl, sift together flour, salt, and baking powder. Add to other ingredients.
6. Mix in vanilla and nuts.
7. Pour into buttered, floured 12-inch x 18-inch pan.
8. Bake 30 to 35 minutes.
9. Cool, cut into squares, and then sprinkle with powdered sugar.

Yield: 2 dozen brownies.

# George Bush (1924- )

## 41st President of the United States

(1989-1993)

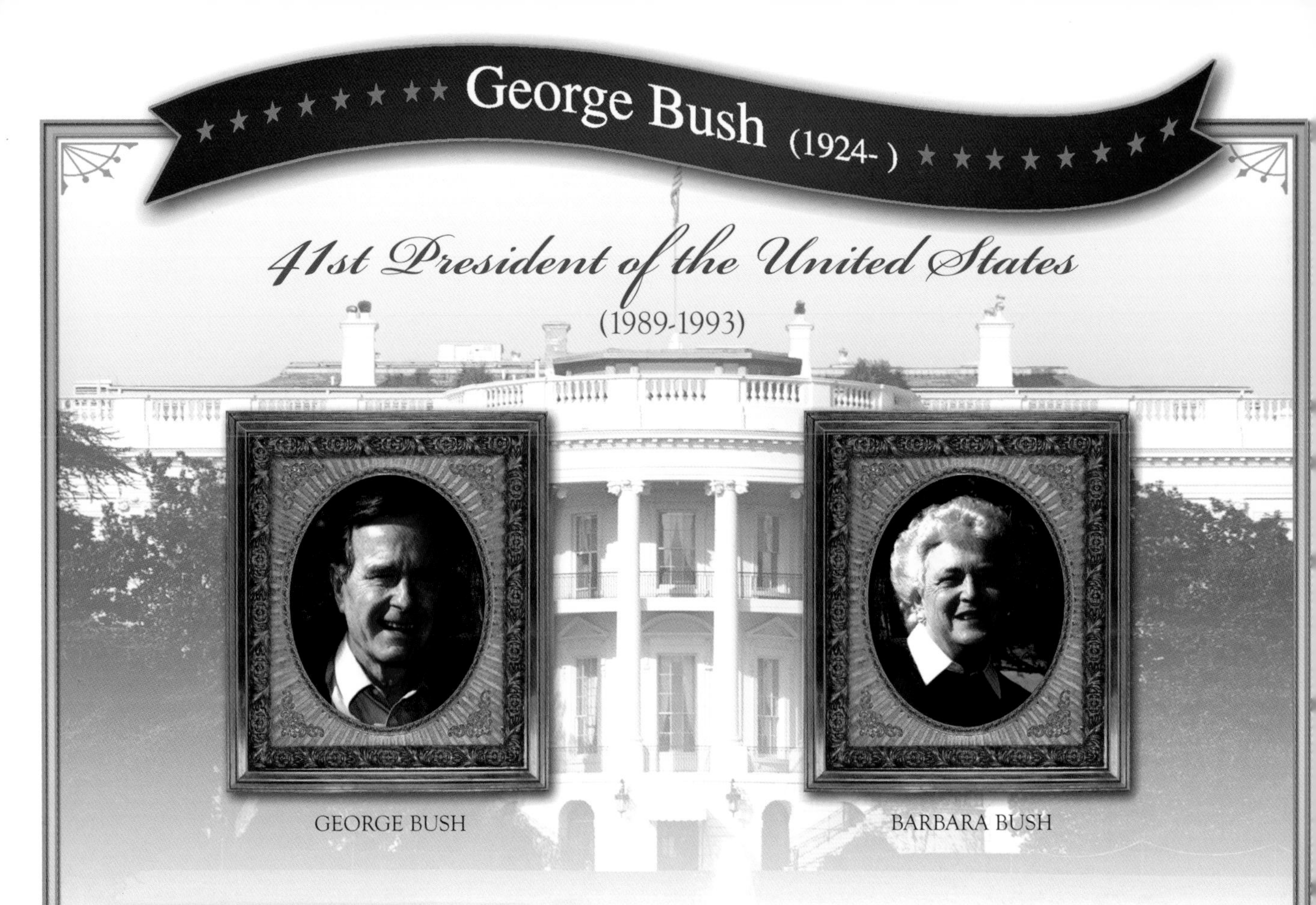

GEORGE BUSH BARBARA BUSH

> ***In 1943 during World War II, George Bush received his pilot wings at the age of 18, becoming the youngest pilot in the Navy.***

Every four years in the United States, election polls try to predict who will win the presidential race. Election "cookie polls" have sprung up as well, becoming an American tradition. Bakeries across the country bake cookies, decorate them with red, white, and blue icing, and top them with the candidate's name, enticing buyers from all parties. Some people buy these cookies to show support for their candidate. Others buy cookies of the candidate they most dislike just to annoy their friends. Still others buy cookies of each contender in a bipartisan spirit. These bakeries report that predicting the next President is easy: he's the candidate with the highest cookie sales.

In 1992, *Family Circle* magazine started a Cookie Cook-off contest between the spouses of the presidential candidates. Readers were asked to "whip up a batch" of each cookie recipe and vote via the Internet. That year President George Bush was running for re-election against Bill Clinton. First Lady Barbara Bush and Hillary Clinton competed with their variation of the American favorite, the chocolate chip cookie. First Lady Barbara used the following recipe for the cookie competition.

# Barbara Bush's Chocolate Chip Cookies

1 cup butter (2 sticks)
1 cup granulated sugar
1 cup light brown sugar, packed
2 eggs
2 cups flour
1 tsp. baking soda
1 tsp. salt
2 cups quick-cooking rolled oats
2 tsp. vanilla
One 12-ounce package chocolate chips

1. Preheat oven to 350°.
2. In a large bowl, mix together butter and sugars.
3. Add eggs and beat well.
4. In another bowl, sift flour, soda, and salt and add to butter mixture.
5. Add oats, vanilla, and chocolate chips.
6. Mix together well and drop by tablespoon onto ungreased cookie sheet.
7. Bake for 10 minutes.

*First Lady Barbara Bush established the Foundation for Family Literacy, supporting programs in which parents and children learn to read together.*

Yield: 3 dozen cookies.

Now that you've tried Barbara Bush's chocolate chip cookie, check out Hillary Clinton's chocolate chip cookie and find the answer to the Cookie Cook-off contest.

# Gingerbread Men Cookies

*Barbara Bush is particularly known for the gingerbread cookies she bakes at Christmas. When guests visited President and First Lady Bush during the holidays, the Bushes gave them cookies off the Christmas tree to take home in little sacks. Every year gingerbread men cookies also hung on the Christmas tree in President Bush's personal office.*

1/2 cup butter (1 stick)
3/4 cup sugar
1 egg, beaten
1/4 cup molasses, light or dark
Juice of 1 lemon
3 1/2 to 4 cups flour
1/2 tsp. salt
1 tsp. soda
1 tsp. cinnamon
1 tsp. ginger
Raisins, enough for decoration
Decorator candies
Decorator icing

1. Preheat oven to 350°.
2. In a large bowl, cream butter and sugar.
3. Beat in egg.
4. Add molasses and lemon juice to creamed mixture.
5. In another bowl, combine dry ingredients and blend into creamed mixture.
6. Chill dough about 1 hour or until stiff enough to handle.
7. Work with half of dough at a time. Store the remainder in refrigerator.
8. Roll dough to 1/4 to 1/8-inch thickness between two pieces of wax paper.
9. Cut with a 4- or 7-inch gingerbread man cutter and remove excess dough.
10. Place greased cookie sheet on top of gingerbread men. Invert sheet and remove wax paper.
11. Press raisins into dough for eyes and nose and decorate as desired with decorator candies.
12. Bake for 10 minutes.
13. Cool 1 minute; remove cookies to rack to finish cooling. Trim with decorator icing.

Yield: Varies with the size of cookie cutter. About a dozen 6-inch gingerbread men.

# Barbara Bush's Original Scotch Shortbread

2 cups sifted flour
1/4 tsp. baking powder
1/4 tsp. salt
1 cup butter (2 sticks)
3/4 cup sifted powdered sugar
2 Tbsp. granulated sugar

1. Preheat oven to 350°.
2. In a small bowl, sift flour with baking powder and salt.
3. In a separate bowl, cream butter and powdered sugar until light and fluffy.
4. Gradually add flour. Mix well.
5. Refrigerate dough until chilled, about 45 minutes.
6. Press dough into an ungreased 8 x 8-inch baking pan.
7. Prick top of dough with fork. Sprinkle with granulated sugar.
8. Bake for 35 to 40 minutes or until top is lightly browned.
9. Cut into 16 squares while warm.

Yield: 16 squares.

These delicate squares tantalize with the rich taste of butter. When I bake a *Presidential Cookies* sampler, I always include this shortbread as one of the Executive Office cookie treasures.

# William J. Clinton (1946- )

## 42nd President of the United States

(1993-2001)

WILLIAM CLINTON

HILLARY CLINTON

> *As a teenager, President Clinton shook the hand of his idol—President John F. Kennedy.*
>
> *President Clinton is the first and only President to be a Rhodes Scholar, attending Oxford University in England.*

President Bill and First Lady Hillary Clinton replaced the frequent French fare of White House dining with the finest in regional American food. The typical American oatmeal cookie and the chocolate chip cookie were the First Family's favorite grabs. The Clintons also continued holiday hospitality at the White House by offering cookies to guests who visited during the Christmas season. During the holidays, more than 100,000 cookies were baked for visitors.

In *Family Circle* magazine's Cookie Cook-off contest, wives of presidential candidates vie for the best cookie recipe. To date, sweet presidential success has been the outcome for the contest winner's husband. Readers who bake the recipes also enjoy the tasty "bake and vote" experience. In 1992, Hillary Clinton and Barbara Bush were the Cook-off contenders. Each competed with her best chocolate chip cookie recipe. Hillary Clinton was declared the

*Hillary Rodham Clinton is the only First Lady to be elected Senator after leaving the White House.*

*Family Circle* magazine winner. Bill Clinton then went on to win the presidency. In 1996, First Lady Clinton's Chocolate Chip Cookie recipe went up against the Pecan Roll Cookies of Elizabeth Dole, wife of candidate Bob Dole. First Lady Hillary Clinton won, and again the election mirrored the Cookie Cook-off poll results. President Bill Clinton was re-elected for a second term.

Following is the *Family Circle* Cookie Cook-off winning recipe for First Lady Hillary Rodham Clinton.

# Hillary Rodham Clinton's Original Chocolate Chip Cookies

1 1/2 CUPS FLOUR
1 TSP. SALT
1 TSP. BAKING SODA
1 CUP SHORTENING
1 CUP BROWN SUGAR, PACKED
1/2 CUP GRANULATED SUGAR
1 TSP. VANILLA
2 EGGS
2 CUPS OLD-FASHIONED ROLLED OATS
ONE 12-OUNCE PACKAGE SEMISWEET CHOCOLATE CHIPS

1. Preheat oven to 350°.
2. Grease baking sheets.
3. Combine flour, salt, and baking soda.
4. In a separate bowl, beat together butter, sugars, and vanilla until creamy.
5. Add eggs, beating until light and fluffy.
6. Gradually beat in flour mixture and rolled oats.
7. Stir in chocolate chips.
8. Drop batter by well-rounded teaspoon onto greased baking sheets.
9. Bake 8 to10 minutes or until golden.
10. Cool cookies on sheets on wire rack for 2 minutes. Remove cookies to wire rack to cool completely.

YIELD: 7 DOZEN COOKIES.

# Dinner

*On the occasion of the visit of*
*The Right Honorable*
*The Prime Minister of the United Kingdom*
*of Great Britain and Northern Ireland*
*and Mrs. Blair*

*Honey Mango Glazed Chicken*
*Spicy Vegetable "Noodles"*
*Herb Tuile*

*Grilled Salmon Fillet "Mignon"*
*Seared Portobello Mushroom*
*Tomato Shallot Fondue*
*Baby Vegetables and Balsamic Reduction*

*Marinated Fresh Mozzarella*
*Roasted Artichokes and Basil Tomatoes*
*Salad of Mache and Arugula*
*Lemon Oregano Dressing*

*"Strawberries and Cream"*
*Devonshire Sauce*
*Brandy Snaps Shortbread*
*Honey Nougat Chocolate Fudge*

NEWTON *Chardonnay "Unfiltered" 1995*
SWANSON *Sangiovese 1995*
MUMM Napa Valley *"DVX" 1993*

*The White House*
*Thursday, February 5, 1998*

Cookies aren't meant just for the cookie jar. This elegant White House dinner, hosted by President and Mrs. Clinton, featured two delicious cookies, Brandy Snaps and Shortbread.

## 43rd President of the United States

(2001- )

GEORGE W. BUSH

LAURA BUSH

According to First Lady Laura Bush, President George W. Bush loves gingerbread cookies baked by his mother, Barbara Bush.

When the President and First Lady were newly married, they received gingerbread cookies by mail from Barbara Bush to hang on their Christmas tree. They continued hanging cookies at Christmas. Before becoming President, the then-Governor Bush of Texas saw to it that cookies hung in the reception room and on the tree at the Governor's Mansion.

In election year 2000, First Lady Laura Bush entered a favorite cookie in *Family Circle* magazine's Cookie Cook-off contest. In the contest, the wives of the presidential candidates compete against each other with their best cookie recipes. This contest has become a pre-election "bake and taste" poll. The magazine's readers bake the cookies and vote for their favorite recipe via the Internet. That year, the Texas Governor's Mansion Cowboy Cookies of Laura Bush won against the Ginger Snaps of Tipper Gore, wife of incumbent Vice President

*When George W. Bush became the 43rd President of the United States in 2001, he joined John Quincy Adams in the distinction of having a father who was also a U.S. President.*

Al Gore. The Cook-off contest winner's husband has always won the presidency. Sure enough, George W. Bush became the 43rd President.

Texas Governor's Mansion Cowboy Cookies reflect the Lone Star background of the President and First Lady. They both grew up in Texas and still maintain their home in Crawford for visits when away from the White House.

In the tradition that everything from Texas is large, Texas Governor's Mansion Cowboy Cookies are mega cookies, huge in size and taste.

# Texas Governor's Mansion Cowboy Cookies

3 cups flour
1 Tbsp. baking powder
1 Tbsp. baking soda
1 Tbsp. ground cinnamon
1 tsp. salt
1 1/2 cups butter (3 sticks), at room temperature
1 1/2 cups granulated sugar
1 1/2 cups light brown sugar, packed
3 eggs
1 Tbsp. vanilla
3 cups semisweet chocolate chips
3 cups old-fashioned rolled oats
2 cups sweetened flake coconut
2 cups chopped pecans (8 ounces)

1. Preheat oven to 350°.
2. Mix flour, baking powder, baking soda, cinnamon, and salt in a bowl.
3. In an 8-quart bowl, beat butter on medium speed for 1 minute until smooth and creamy.
4. Gradually beat in sugars to combine for 2 minutes.
5. Add eggs, one at a time, beating after each.
6. Beat in vanilla.
7. Stir in flour mixture until just combined.
8. Add chocolate chips, oats, coconut, and pecans.
9. For each cookie, drop 1/4 cup dough onto ungreased baking sheets, spacing 3 inches apart.*
10. Bake 17 to 29 minutes, until edges are lightly browned; rotate sheets halfway through (after 10 minutes).
11. Remove cookies to a rack to cool.

* For 6 dozen small cookies, use 2 tablespoons dough for each. Bake at 350°F for 15 to 18 minutes.

*Laura Bush is the only First Lady to deliver an entire presidential radio address.*

*As a former teacher and librarian, First Lady Laura Bush took the opportunity to share her love of reading by hosting the first National Book Festival in Washington D.C., in 2001.*

YIELD: 3 DOZEN COOKIES.

These huge cookies do Texas proud with their chunky mounds of the richest and best ingredients. They are among the most popular presidential cookies I've baked for friends. I search for my BIGGEST bowl to mix up the ingredients and use my ice cream scoop to shape each cookie. Since the recipe makes lots of very big cookies, I usually freeze half the dough so that I can bake more cookies at another time.

# Notes

*Happy Baking*

# Acknowledgments

The author is grateful to so many friends, associates, and organizations for your invaluable assistance with this book. You were exceptionally helpful, enthusiastic, and gracious to provide materials for *Presidential Cookies.* Special thanks to all the dedicated cookie taste-testers.

Barbara Bloom and Bill Windt
Dan Bode
Lori Christensen
Sue Collins
Connie DaMant
Lynne Gomez-Yim and Chantel Yim
Staff at Greenhaven Veterinary Hospital
Dana Harvey
Kristin Heidelbach
Tim Jordan
Clint Kim
Kerry Kraus
Jim Mullany
The Neumann Family: Ann, Tom, Anyssa, and Ambria
Lisa Nixon
Kathy Osborne
Dan Poynter
Eleanor Roosevelt II
Sacramento Public Library
Marie Saur
The Shows Family: Terry, Tracy, Hannah, Grace, and Nicholas
Cindy Stone
Marcia Wieder
Jill Withrow

Adams National Historic Park
President Chester A. Arthur State Historic Site
The James Buchanan Foundation
George Bush Presidential Library and Museum
Jimmy Carter Library
Clinton Presidential Materials Project
President Calvin Coolidge State Historic Site

Dwight D. Eisenhower Library
The Gerald R. Ford Presidential Library and Museum
James A. Garfield National Historic Site
Ulysses S. Grant National Historic Site
President Benjamin Harrison Home
Grouseland, Home of William Henry Harrison
Rutherford B. Hayes Presidential Center
The Hermitage, The Home of Andrew Jackson
Herbert Hoover Presidential Library and Museum
Monticello/Thomas Jefferson Foundation
Andrew Johnson National Historical Site
Lyndon Baines Johnson Library and Museum
John F. Kennedy Library and Museum
Library of Congress
Lincoln Home National Historic Site
The Lincoln Museum
James Madison's Montpelier
The James Madison Museum
Marblehead Magazine
Ash Lawn-Highland, Home of James Monroe
James Monroe Museum and Memorial Library
Mount Vernon Ladies' Association
National First Ladies' Library
Richard Nixon Library and Birthplace
The Pierce Manse
James K. Polk Memorial Association
Ronald Reagan Presidential Library
Franklin D. Roosevelt Presidential Library and Museum
Theodore Roosevelt Collection, The Houghton Library, Harvard University
Theodore Roosevelt Inaugural National Historic Site
Sagamore Hill National Historic Site, Theodore Roosevelt's Home
The Sequoia Presidential Yacht Foundation
The Smithsonian
William Howard Taft National Historic Site
Harry S. Truman Presidential Museum and Library
Harry S. Truman National Historic Site, National Park Service
Sherwood Forest Plantation, Home of President John Tyler
Martin Van Buren National Historic Site
Vermont Division for Historic Preservation
George Washington's Mount Vernon Estate & Gardens
The White House
The White House Historical Association
Woodrow Wilson House

# References


Cannon, Poppy and Patricia Brooks. *The Presidents' Cookbook.* New York: Funk and Wagnalls, 1968.

Clinton, Hillary Rodham. *An Invitation to the White House.* New York: Simon & Shuster, 2000.

Donald, Kathleen E. and John Almon Waterhouse, eds. *Coolidge-Country Cookbook: Early Recipes of the Coolidge Family, Their Plymouth Notch, Vermont Neighbors and Friends.* Plymouth: Friends of the Calvin Coolidge Memorial Foundation, 1988.

Editors of American Heritage, The Magazine of History. *The American Heritage Cookbook.* New York: American Heritage Press, 1964.

Eisenhower Library. *Eisenhower Recipes.* National Archives and Records Administration, 1995.

Ervin, Janet Halliday. *The White House Cookbook.* Chicago: Follett Publishing Company, 1964.

Glasse, Hannah. *First Catch Your Hare: The Art of Cookery Made Plain & Easy (facsimile).* Devon: Prospect Books, 1995.

Haller, Henry with Virginia Aronson. *The White House Family Cookbook.* New York: Random House, 1987.

Healy, Diana Dixon. *America's First Ladies.* New York: Antheneum Macmillian Publishing Company, 1988.

Hechtlinger, Adelaide. *The Seasonal Hearth.* New York: The Overlook Press, 1977.

Hess, Karen. *Martha Washington's Booke of Cookery and Booke of Sweetmeats.* New York: Columbia University Press, 1995.

Ichord, Loretta Frances. *Hasty Pudding, Johnnycakes, and Other Good Stuff.* Brookfield: The Millbrook Press, 1998.

*In the Kitchen with Bill.* Kansas City: Andrews and McMeel Universal Press Syndicate Co., 1996.

Jones, Taffy. *Who Is Uncle Sam?* Lanham: Maryland Historical Press, 1991.

Kane, Joseph Nathan. *Facts About the Presidents.* New York: The H.W. Wilson Co., 1993.

Kimball, Marie. *Thomas Jefferson's Cook Book.* Charlottesville: University Press of Virginia, 1999.

Klapthor, Margaret Brown. *The First Ladies.* Washington, D.C.: White House Historical Association, 1983.

—. *Official White House China.* New York: Smithsonian Institution Press, 1975.

Kodik, Judith E., ed. *Monroe Family Recipes.* Ash Lawn-Highland, 1999.

Means, Marianne. *The Woman in the White House.* New York: Random House, 1963.

*Montpelier Hospitality.* Montpelier Station: The Montpelier Foundation, 2002.

Nesbitt, Henrietta. *White House Diary.* New York: Doubleday & Co., Inc., 1948.

Parents' Magazine Enterprises. *The First Ladies' Cook Book.* New York: Parents' Magazine Press, 1969.

President Benjamin Harrison Foundation, Inc. *The President Harrison Home Recipes.* Olathe: Cookbook Publishers, Inc., 1993.

Recht Penner, Lucille. *The Colonial Cookbook.* New York: Hastings House, 1976.

Russoli, Edward and Candace. *Ike the Cook.* Allentown: Benedettini Books, 1990.

Rysavy, Francois and Frances Spatz Leighton. *A Treasury of White House Cooking.* New York: G.P. Putnam's Sons, 1972.

Sandburg, Carl. *Abraham Lincoln, The Prairie Years II.* US, Great Britain, and Canada: Harcourt, Brace and World, Inc., 1925.

Smith, Marie. *Entertaining in the White House.* Washington, D.C.: Acropolis Books, 1967.

Sullivan, George. *Facts and Fun About the Presidents.* New York: Scholastic Inc., 1987.

Editors of Time-Life Books. Dawn of the century: 1900-1910, Alexandria, VA: Time-Life Books, 1998.

The Founders, Washington Committee for Historic Mount Vernon. *The Mount Vernon Cookbook.* Mount Vernon: The Mount Vernon Ladies' Association of the Union, 2002.

*The James K. Polk Cookbook.* Columbia: The James K. Polk Memorial Auxiliary. 1978.

Ungano, Susan Kelliher. "Why Traditions Matter." *Family Circle.* New York: G J USA Publishing, Dec.18, 2001. pp 102-106.

Ziemann, Hugo and F.L. Gillette. *White House Cookbook, Revised and Updated Centennial Edition.* Minneapolis: Chronimed Publishing, 1996.

## Electronic Sources


"10 Things Every Yankee Doodle Dandy Should Know." Microsoft Corp. Encarta. 23 Aug. 2001.
<http://encarta.msn.com/list/unclesamposter.asp>

American Presidents: Life Portraits. 1999. 23 Aug. 2001.
<http://www.americanpresidents.org/presidents/president.asp?PresidentNumber=18>

Aucella, Frank J. "Re: Request for information." E-mail to the author. 21 Dec. 2000.

Bartram, Graham. Vice President of the United States. 2000. 6 Nov. 2000.
<http://www.fotw.ca/flags/us-vpres.html>

"Batter Up: Would-Be First Ladies Enter Cook-Off." 2000. ABC News. 7 Aug. 2000.
<http:// www.abcnews.go.com/sections/politics/DailyNews/cookie000619.html>

Berk, Pam. "Authentic Berks County Recipes." Berk's Web Berks County, Pennsylvania. 12 Apr. 2000.
<http://www.berksweb.com/recipe_board/messages/6346.html>

Bush, Laura. "Cookie Cook-Off: Bush." 2000. ABC News. 10 Dec. 2000.
<http://abcnews.go.com/onair/goodmorningamerica/recipes/gma000620_bushcookies.html>

Capps, Mike. "Re: Information Request." E-mail to the author. 26 Dec. 2000.

Comito, Mark. Fax to the author. 21 Dec. 2000.

Database of American Presidents. 22 Sept. 2002.
<http://odur.let.rug.nl/~usa/P/index.htm>

Davis, Susan E. "Thirteen Fun Facts About Ice Cream." 2001. DrSpock. 1 Nov. 2002.
<http://www.drspock.com/article/0%2C1510%2C5941%2C00.html>

George Bush Presidential Library and Museum. 15. Feb. 2000.
<http://bushlibrary.tamu.edu/>

George Washington's Mount Vernon Estate & Gardens. 25 Mar. 2000.
<http://www.mountvernon.org/>

Gojgic, Ljubica. "Election 2000." 2000. post-pazette.com. 24 May 2001.
<http://www.post-gazette.com/election2000/20001031cookies9.asp>

Gundersen, Geir. "Re: Request for information." Fax to the author. 13 Dec. 2000.

Haake, Susan. "Re: Request for information." E-mail to the author. 18 Dec. 2000.

Holzweiss, Robert. "Re: Request for information." E-mail to the author. 11 Dec. 2000.

Lyndon Baines Johnson Library and Museum. 3 July 2001.
<http://www.lbjlib.utexas.edu/johnson/archives.hom/FAQs/Recipes/recipes.asp>

National Archives and Records Administration. 25 Sept. 2001.
<http://www.nara.gov/>

National First Ladies' Library. 13 Aug. 2001.
<http://www.firstladies.org/>

Osborne, Kathy. Telephone conversation with the author. 5 Dec. 2001.

Presidential Sites Idea Network. 24 July 2001.
<http://www.ibiblio.org/lia/president/pressites/>

Presidents of the United States. Internet Public Library. 3 Jan. 2001.
<http://www.ipl.org/ref/POTUS/>

Purdin, Bill. "Re: Information request." E-mail to the author. 29 Dec. 2000.

Refdesk.com. 9 Sept. 2002.
<http://www.refdesk.com/>

Rutherfold B. Hayes Presidential Center. 6 June 2001.
<http://www.rbhayes.org/>

Sequoia Presidential Yacht Foundation. 8 Nov. 2001.
<http://www.casenet.com/travel/wasdcpresyacht.htm>

Sewell, Cate. Fax to the author. 12 Dec. 2000.

Spencer, Laura. "Re: Gingerbread Cookie Recipe." E-mail to the author. 2 Jan. 2002.

Stalling, Kristen. "Re: Request for information." Fax to the author. 11 Jan. 2001.

"Sweet Memories: 100 Years of Cookies." Good Housekeeping. 1999. 20 July 2001.
<http://goodhousekeeping.com/gh/eatwell/cooking/c9ghco16.htm>

Taylor, Barry. "Yankee Doodle." Yankee Doodle. 8 Sept. 2002.
<http://www.contemplator.com/america/ydoodle.html>

The American Experience. PBS Television. 2001-2002. 8 Sept. 2002.
<http://www.pbs.org/wgbh/amex/>

The American President Series Website. 23 July 2001.
<http://www.americanpresident.org/introduction_body.htm>

The Eisenhower Presidential Library. 7 July 2001.
<http://www.eisenhower.utexas.edu/vcgftcat.pdf>

The Eleanor Roosevelt Center at Val-Kill. 39 Nov. 2001.
<http://www.ervk.org/>

The First Ladies. 7 May. 2001.
<http://www.firstladies.org/>

The Home of James Madison's Montpelier. 18 Oct. 2001.
<http://www.montpelier.org/>

The Library of Virginia. 12 Jan. 2001.
<http://www.lva.lib.va.us/>

The Lincoln Museum. 25 Feb. 2001.
<http://www.thelincolnmuseum.org/index.asp>

The White House. 12 Jan. 2001.
<www.whitehouse.gov>

US Flag of the United States. 8 July 2001.
<http://www.usflag.org/the.pledge.of.allegiance.htm>

Van Geertruyden, Brooke. Office of Barbara Bush. Letter to the author. 22 Jan. 2002.

Weltner, Linda. "Black Joe." Marblehead Magazine. 23. Aug. 2002.
<http://www.legendinc.com/Pages/MarbleheadNet/MM/Articles/BlackJoe.html>

White House Historical Association. 9 June 2001.
<http://www.whitehousehistory.org/>

Williams, Crystal. Letter to the author. 1 Mar. 2001.

Winters, Rosie. "The US White House Easter Egg Roll." Not Just For Kids. 1995-99. 8 Aug. 2002.
<http://www.night.net/easter/eggroll.html-ssi>

# Image Credits

George Washington. Pastel portrait by James Sharples, c. 1796. Courtesy of the Mount Vernon Ladies' Association. p. 15

Martha Washington. Pastel portrait by James Sharples, c. 1796 date unknown. Courtesy of the Mount Vernon Ladies' Association. p. 15

*West View.* Oil on canvas attributed to Edward Savage, c. 1792. Courtesy of the Mount Vernon Ladies' Association. p. 18

Mount Vernon Kitchen. Courtesy of the Mount Vernon Ladies' Association. p. 18

John Adams. Courtesy of the Library of Congress. p. 19

Abigail Adams. Courtesy of the Library of Congress. p. 19

Thomas Jefferson. 1858 James L. Dick copy of Rembrandt Peale's 1805 second life portrait of Jefferson, Courtesy of the Monticello/Thomas Jefferson Foundation, Inc. p. 22

James Madison by Vanderlyn. The White House Collection, Courtesy White House Historical Association. p. 24

Dolley Madison by Stuart. The White House Collection, Courtesy White House Historical Association. p. 24

*A View of the Presidents house in the city of Washington after the conflagration of the 24th August 1814.* Courtesy of the Library of Congress. p. 25

Miniature of James Monroe, ca. 1796 by Louis Sene. Courtesy of the James Monroe Museum and Memorial Library, Fredericksburg, Virginia. p. 27

Miniature of Elizabeth Monroe, ca. 1796 by Louis Sene. Courtesy of Ash-Highland, home of James Monroe, Charlottesville, Virginia. p. 27

John Quincy Adams. Courtesy of the Library of Congress. p. 30

Louisa Adams. Courtesy of the Library of Congress. p. 30

Andrew Jackson. Courtesy of The Hermitage: Home of President Andrew Jackson, Nashville, TN. p. 32

*President's Levee, or all Creation going to the White House.* Courtesy of the Library of Congress. p. 33

*The Great Cheese Levee.* The White House Collection, Courtesy White House Historical Association. p. 36

Martin Van Buren. Courtesy of the Martin Van Buren National Historic Site, National Park Service. p. 38

William Henry Harrison. Courtesy of the Library of Congress. p. 40

Anna Harrison. Courtesy of the Library of Congress. p. 40

Handwritten recipes of Bess Truman (Fax). Courtesy of the Harry S. Truman National Historic Site, National Park Service. p. 113

Dwight D. Eisenhower. Courtesy of the Dwight D. Eisenhower Library. p. 116

Mamie Eisenhower. Courtesy of the Dwight D. Eisenhower Library. p. 116

John F. Kennedy. Cecil Stoughton, Courtesy of the White House/John Fitzgerald Kennedy Library, Boston, MA. p. 119

Jacqueline Kennedy. Courtesy of the John Fitzgerald Kennedy Library, Boston, MA. p. 119

Lyndon B. Johnson. Photo by Yoichi R. Okamoto, Jan. 9, 1969. Courtesy of the Lyndon Baines Johnson Library and Museum. p. 121

Lady Bird Johnson. Photo by Robert Knudsen, Oct. 20, 1967. Courtesy of the Lyndon Baines Johnson Library and Museum. p. 121

Mrs. Lyndon Johnson's recipes. Courtesy of the Lyndon Baines Johnson Library and Museum. p. 122

Richard M. Nixon. Courtesy of the Richard Nixon Library & Birthplace. p. 125

Patricia Nixon. Courtesy of the Richard Nixon Library & Birthplace. p. 125

*USS Sequoia* photograph and seal. Courtesy of the Sequoia Presidential Yacht Foundation. p. 127

Gerald Ford. Courtesy of the Gerald R. Ford Library. p. 129

Betty Ford. Courtesy of the Gerald R. Ford Library. p. 129

Jimmy Carter. Courtesy of the Jimmy Carter Library. p. 131

Rosalynn Carter. Courtesy of the Jimmy Carter Library. p. 131

Ronald Reagan. Courtesy of the Reagan Library. p. 136

Nancy Reagan. Courtesy of the Reagan Library. p. 136

George Bush. Courtesy of the George Bush Presidential Library. p. 140

Barbara Bush. Courtesy of the George Bush Presidential Library. p. 140

William Clinton. Courtesy of the Clinton Presidential Materials Project. p. 144

Hillary Clinton. Courtesy of the Clinton Presidential Materials Project. p. 144

Clinton White House Dinner Menu. Courtesy of the Clinton Presidential Materials Project. p. 147

George W. Bush. Courtesy of the George Bush Presidential Library. p. 148

Laura Bush. Courtesy of the George Bush Presidential Library. p. 148

# Index

R

## Quick Order Form

Fax orders: **(916) 447-2460** Send this form.

E-mail orders: **contactus@presidentialpublishing.com**
**contactus@presidentialcookies.com**

Telephone orders: Toll-free **1-866-6Baking (1-866-622-5464) or (916) 421-5267**
Have your credit card ready.

Postal orders: Presidential Publishing, PO Box 221834, Sacramento, CA 95822, USA. Telephone: **(916) 421-5267**

Please send _______ copies of *Presidential Cookies* @ **$23.95** per book plus shipping.

Shipping within the US: $4.50 for the first book, $2.50 for each additional book shipped to the same address. California residents add $1.85 sales tax for each book.

Shipping outside of the US: $9 for the first book, $5 for each additional book shipped to the same address. (estimate)

Ordered by ____________________ Company (if any)____________________

Delivery address______________________________________________
(We cannot ship to a P.O. Box)

State____________ Zip Code____________ Country__________________

Telephone # ____________________ E-mail address ____________________

Payment ☐ Check: Make checks payable to **Presidential Publishing**

☐ Credit Card: ☐Visa ☐MasterCard

Card # ______________________________________________________

Name on Card ________________________________ Exp. Date __________
(Please Print)

Amount Authorized $ ____________________

Customer Signature ______________________________________________

**Allow 1 to 2 weeks for delivery.**